IMPACT OF MODERNISATION ON TRIBAL COSTUME

By
Dr. Sonu Mehta
M.Sc., Ph.D.

DISCOVERY PUBLISHING HOUSE PVT. LTD.
NEW DELHI-110 002

Published by:
Tilak Wasan
DISCOVERY PUBLISHING HOUSE PVT. LTD.
4383/4B, Ansari Road, Darya Ganj
New Delhi-110 002 (India)
Phone : +91-11-23279245, 43596064-65
Fax : +91-11-23253475
E-mail : parul.wasan@gmail.com
discoverypublishinghouse@gmail.com
web : www.discoverypublishinggroup.com

***First Edition:* 2013**

ISBN: 978-93-5056-272-7

Impact of Modernisation on Tribal Costume

Printed at:
Dynamic Printers
Delhi

Preface

Costume is the language which tells about nature, culture, status, personality, creativity, interest, and values of any individual. It provides visible index of the homogeneity and the unity of people. Costume includes coiffure and ornaments. Consciously unconsciously, people are at first interested in clothes and ornaments as devices for enhancing the attractiveness of the body, but gradually they develop an interest in clothes lor their own sake.

Costumes adorns the body and enriches its appearance, making a person gorgeous and enchanting besides safeguarding his/her body. Thus costume not only serves the utilitarian purpose of covering the body but also used with special effect to enhance the beauty and elegance of the person.

Whatever, might be the origin of the costume it provides the visible index of the homogeneity and the unity of people. Costume conveys more than mere clothing. It also includes coiffure and ornaments. Coiffure refers to headdress and hairstyle while ornaments are used for decoration of the body parts it includes jewellery, tattooing, body painting etc.

This volume is divided into seven main the life chapters. First chapter deals with the importance and history of costume, second, tells us about the life style of four major tribal groups of Rajasthan i.e. Bhil, Garasia, Damor, and Kathodi. Third chapter includes the present and changing trends of Bhil costume since independence in detail, similarly the fourth, fifth and sixth deals with the Garasia, Damor and Kathodi tribes respectively. The photographs of every is also attached for more clear perception.

I hope this volume will be worthwhile for the scholars, and traditional costume designers. I am greatful to my father Dr. Prakash Mehta who inspired and helped me in the completion of this title. At the same time I am thankful to my mam Dr. Meena Gaur who guided me in the whole research work. I am also thankful to my family members-husband Mr. Sunil Mehta, Daughter Mitali, mother Smt. Yashoda Mehta, sister smt. Sangeeta Mehta, brother Mr. Anurag Mehta for their motivation and moral support.

Dr. Sonu Mehta

Contents

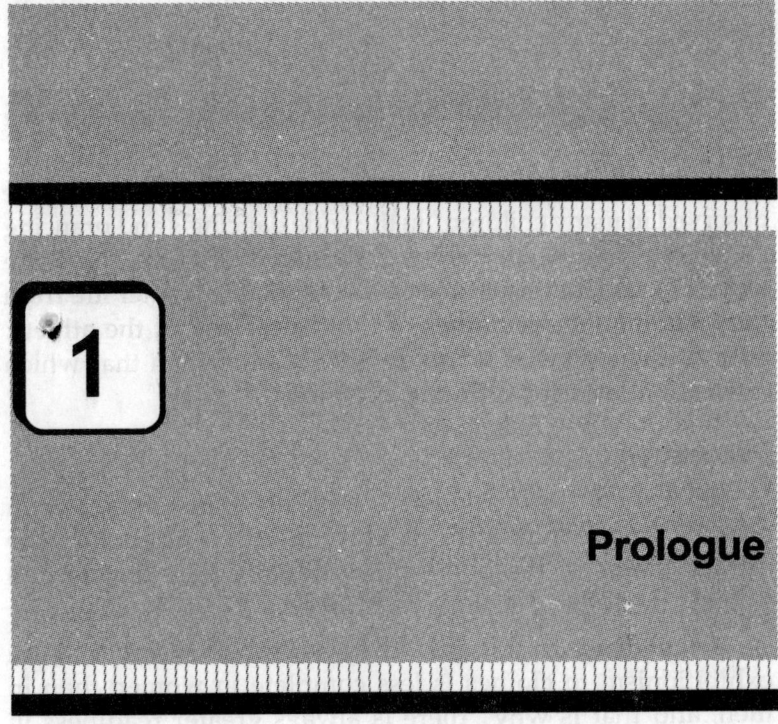

1 Prologue

Clothing is an expression of the person, reflecting personality, way of living, way of thinking and especially, pride in self or family. Thus, clothing should be no more than a tool, an aid in expressing what and who the person is. It is a reflection of one's taste, one's life and one's values.

The primitive people did not wore any clothes. Now the question arises, what happens which compell the human race to wear clothes? There were few reasons due to which people had started wearing clothes these are:

Narcissism

The dress was developed as a result of man's narcissim, that is his pleasure in his own body and his desire to make himself as attractive as possible physically.

Narcissism "Finds a natural expression in the showing off of the naked body and in the demonstration of its powers," declared Dr. John Carl Flugel, one of the first psychologists to become seriously interested in clothes. In his book *The*

Psychology of Clothes, he commented that narcissism can be observed in many children "in the wide dancing's and prancing in which, if allowed, they will indulged..... Much the same kinds of satisfaction are doubtless obtainable in later life from the exhibitionistic activities of the dancer and of the athlete, both of them clad as a rule in alter scanter than that which modesty allows for ordinary occasions".[1]

Decoration

Consciously or unconsciously, people are at just interested in clothes and ornaments as devices for enhancing the attractiveness of the body, but gradually they develop an interest in clothes for their own sake.

According to Flugel, they shift in interest from exhibitionism to clothes is less complete in women than in men, and that is why "there is always greater readiness in women to combine displaced exhibitionism with actual exposure, as in the decollete."[2]

Traditionally, people are more tolerant of narcissism in women than in men, and this difference is revealed in clothes. The western world especially has idealized the rounded female form and has been some what critical of the male physique with its greater angularity, hairiness, and muscular development.

Among primitive peoples interest in body decoration seems to be the Chief motive for dress. Some tribes paint their bodies or tattoo on themselves an all-over pattern to enhance their own physical attractiveness.

Tattooing and painting have also been used to show tribal connections and rank within the tribe. Another decorative device adopted by some savage tribes is scarring that is, making cuts on the body, then working clay into the cuts so the flesh will heal in welts.[3]

Very early, apparently, men and women began to use shells, bones and similar ornaments to hang upon themselves trophies of the hunt and of tribal wars also provided many decorative ornaments which increased the wearer's prestige. The primitive both male and female, liked to wear rings on fingers, ankles, neck, *waistand hips.*"[4]

In some primitive tribes only the women wore clothes, and then usually only after she was married to indicate that she was the property of her mate. In the tribes only the harlot was clothed. Jody's wedding ring had its origin in metal rings often worn around or neck to indicate such ownership and sometimes to protect the wearer from evil spirits.

Protection

As the human race is believed to have originated in tropical parts of the earth, man probably used body coverings for protection somewhat belatedly, and most likely only as he moved into less equable areas. Then he found that coverings made of plant fibers and skins not only were decorative best also protected him from heat and cold, and from insects, thorny underbush, and stony tertian. Coverings also made it possible for him to be active when most of the lower animals had to withdraw into shelters.

Protection from the evil spirits which primitive man believed were all around him was another, but probably a secondary, reason for his wearing clothes and amulets or charms. Hiding his sex organs, he believed would keep demons from making him sterile. Women wore their aprons and hip clothes in pat for the same reasons.[5]

Clothes to Attract the Opposite Sex

Clothing originated in n an's desire to play up his own physical charms and make himself more attractive to others, especially to the opposite sex. Among savages, body decoration starts at or near the genital organs and often issued in connection with a ceremony celebrating the attainment of some stage in sexual development, as the arrival of puberty or the selection of a mate.[6]

According to Flugel, "The ultimate purpose of clothes, and often ended their overt and conscious purpose, is to add to the sexual attractiveness to the opposite sex and the envy of rivals of the same sex.": Sexual life, both among the primitive and among the civilized, supplies the strongest motive for wearing clothes.[7]

In any one season today's designs of fashion characteristically select one or more of seven "themes" to play up in women's clothes: the neck or the breasts, the waist or he abdomen, the hips, the buttocks, the legs, the ears, or the length or circumference of the body itself. James Laver, the British fashion historian, and some psychiatrists call these "Shifting erogenous zones"—that is, shifting areas that have sex appeal. Designers emphasize their selected theme and cover most other parts until men's interest in that theme has would, then they cover it and emphasize some other part.[8]

In earlier periods the tight corset had a similar objective. Constructing the waist emphasized breasts, abdomen, and buttocks; it also forced women to breathe from the upper part of the lungs, giving breasts a respiratory movement and added allurement to the opposite sex.

The part of the body selected for fashion emphasis is always either bared or emphasized by drawing the clothes tightly around it as a "second skin", or by exaggerating it through paddling.[10]

Modesty

Modesty is a definite motive for clothes, but only a secondary one, today's social scientists believe that the urge towards modesty apparently developed after the wearing of clothes had become habitual. Children are not born with this age. They are naturally bashful, but they have no sense of shame at the exposure of any part of their bodies, no feeling that some pats of the body are not ice. Savages who wear clothes do so with no apparent idea of modesty. As we have already noted, they are likely stead to shift from nakedness to clothes for sexual stimulation.

"The sense of modesty is merely a habit, not an instinct", the insists than anthropologist E. Adamson Hoebel. A person whose sense of modesty is ocetranged by a behavioural situation contrary to custom gets a terrific shock, both emotionally and physically. Fear and anxiety are aroused by his lifelong feeling that those who do not follow the customary behaviour pattern will be punished by social or perhaps even supernatural agencies.[11]

To Show Place in Society

From the time that man first adopted clothes, he has used them in pat to show his place in society. This motive, later declares, has always figured as apparently as the motive, of self decoration to attract the opposite sex. He labels the two drives hierarchy and reduction and comments. "Fashion breeds on reduction and thrives on snobbery."[12]

The urge to imitate the envied so as to reach their status make impelling motives for following fashion leaders. The desire to belong, to be accepted as apart of some social group, also provides a powerful motive for dressing in the mode, especially during adolescence. Most adolescents, throughout their high school and college days, are interested not so much in standing out from the crowd through superiority of dress as in being as much like all the rest as possible.[1]

Clothes help to crystalline and maintain class distinctions in any society. In some parts of the world they distinguish the aristocracy from the peasants, the white-collar from the blue-collar workers.[14]

Comfort

Comfort in dress today rates higher than it has in the past, especially for recreation and for casual living. In general the people wants, garments that do not restrict movement, fabrics that feel good to the skin, warmth in winter, and coolness in summer within limits.

For formal and semiformal occasions, when the demands of comfort and of fashion clash, comfort is likely to rate a poor second. This is especially in case of adolescent and young ones. They gradually give first preference to the fashionable clothing rather than comfortable clothing.

Whatever, might be the origin of the costuming provides the visible index of the homogeneity and the unity of people. Costume conveys more than clothing. It also includes coiffure and ornaments, coiffure refers to headdress and hair style, while ornaments are used for decoration of the body parts it includes jewellery, tattooing, body painting, etc.

As with the passage of time the change in the costume is widely visible. Thus with every new era we will find change in the clothing of male and female.

Pre-Historic to First Century B.D.

Religious texts from India's prehistory in the *Rig Veda* and the *Upanishads,* tell us about early literary references to fabric, relating to nearly 3,000 years ago, tell us about the subcontinent's superiority as a producer of textile, and as master dyer to the world. They are some of the only clues left to give evidence of India's creative design history on its textile as none of the wealth of ancient Indian textiles has survived the vagaries of its gruelling, alternative wet and dry monsoon climate. Due to this scarcity of evidence a few biodegradable fragments of woven plant and animal fibre remain. It is counterbalanced by other archaeological finds and passages in literature, which lead any investigation into India textiles. The manufacture of sophisticated Costumes and textiles and their various designs on them is an ancient as Indian civilization.

India is the home of cotton and it was woven here since prehistoric times. When the Romans and Greeks, whose ships reached the shores of India across the Indian Ocean, first saw cotton, they described it as wool that grew on trees.

The cloth fragments, as well as terracotta spindles and Bronze needless found at the site, are evidence that the cultivation of cotton, spinning, weaving, and printing in India were at least as old as *Mohenjo-daro.*[16]

Buddhist literature has many references to the magnificant cotton spinners and weavers of *Kashi* (Allahabad). The fabric was so finely woven that oil could not penetrate the cloth. Spinning was the work of women. Cotton cloths were washed, calendared, starched and perfumed. We can also see Inlay instances of ornamental woven fabrics in the *Ajanta* frescoes. Here, in the themes illustraining the stores of the *Jataka,* some of the costumes showed that the textiles used were of the finest quality, with excellence of weave texture and decorative motif, showing geese, flowers, scrolls and geometrical patterns.

The excavations at *Mohenjo-daro* have revealed some details about Indian costume and the materials from which cloth was manufactured. An actual piece of cotton has been discovered which shows that cotton was known to the people of *Sindh* four thousand five hundred years back. It is also possible that wool was used for warmer textiles. Our knowledge of the customs of Mohenjo-daro people is scanty as naked figures preponderate. A shawl is worn by a male figure covering the left shoulder and passed under the right arm. It is difficult to say that what was under the shawl, but the heroes and deities wear a strip of cotton on their loins. Some very rare figurines are depicted wearing kilt or drawers. The hair was tied with a woven fillet.

The woven *sari* terminated well above the knees was always fastened with girdles and in one case with kamarband has also been seen. The narrow strip of cloth used as sari at Mohenjo-daro very much resembles the nivi mentioned in the *Vedic* literature. Fan-shaped head-dresses were worn by men and women who had sometimes pannier-like projections and round the head helped to support them; cap was also worn by a few figurines.

The skins of the animals were worn by the Gods and *Munis,* and aboriginal tribes. Goat and antelope skins were preferred. *Ksauma,* most probably lien, cloth manufactured from the bark of tree. The work of weaving was entrusted to women-folk. *Vedic* Indians were also fond of beautiful garments. The clothes were also well-fitting they were often decorated with borders or embroidered with patterns in gold. White cloth was preferred, while some women used dyed cloth.[17]

The *Vedic* Indians wore three garments; loin-cloth sometimes having long and unwoven fringe, and an over garment generally consisted of a wrapper or sometimes a jacket, bodice or cloak was worn by dancing girls. The turban was worn by the Rajas and also sometimes by women. Shoes were not mentioned in the early *Vedic* literature though foot-fasteners and foot-guards used in battle fields were mentioned in the *Rigveda,* The shoes were first mentioned in the *Yajurveda* and were worn at the ritual. They were manufactured from boar or antelope skins.

In the next period which may tentatively cover the period between 642-413 B.C., material for Indian clothing is to be found in the *Sutra* literature, *Jataka* stories and *Vinaya Pitaka.* In this period the professions of embroider and weaving were considered low, which must have been due to these professions being taken up by the non-Aryans, as in the *Vedic* age no such stigma was attached to these professions.[18]

Cotton was greatly cultivated in this age and are gold about cotton fields near Varanasi. Fine threads rolled in balls were in demand, and bow for carding is also mentioned. Varanasi, during the life of Buddha, seems to have been the chief center of the manufacture of cotton cloth, and it is said that the mortal remains of a world ruler were covered with it. The texture of cloth produced at Varanasi was fine, and this fineness and smoothness were obtained by skilled weavers and spinners, and bleaching was perfect due to the softness of the water. Varanasi was also famous for its silk manufacture and up to this day it is one of the leading silk manufacturing centers in India.

Linen was common; blankets were also produced from a mixture of fiber and wool. For woolen cloths of all varieties the term *kambala* is used in Buddhist literature. The Gandhara country produced fine shawls; besides the above-mentioned varieties, cloths were manufactured from hemp, grass, bark, wood, human hair, feather, etc. Skins of lions, tiger leopard, cow and deer, etc., were used for bedding and clothes. In the *Madhyadesa* the skins of various species of cats, etc., and in the *Daksinapatha* the skins of rams, goats, etc. were used for clothing. The patterned and dyed garment, with beautiful borders was common.[20]

The history of Indian customers in the Maurya, Sunga and early Andhra period can be traced from sculptures, terracott's, and partly from literature. We know on the basis of Kautilya that there was a separate department of state & superintendent where thread, cloths, coats and ropes were manufacture.[21] The materials employed for the manufacture of cloth were cotton, silk, wool, hemp, fiber, etc. Cotton was grown, and the skins, furs and beautiful woolen cloths were imported from China.

The dress was simple *dhoti* or loin-cloth fastened to the waist with *kamarband* generally tied in bow-shaped knot with a *patka* at time hanging in between the legs, and *dupatta* or turban. It was remarkable that *dhoti* in later Maurya and Sunga periods was very beautifully pleated, and the patkas were decorated with beautiful patterns, tassels, etc. The women also wore *saris* with kamarbands and *patkas,* and elaborate veils. In past the few Mayuryan sculptures and reliefs of Bharhut depict a fashionable society where even simple garments were worn in such a way as to attract attention.

For the history of Indian costumes in this period there is ample material in the Gandhara and Mathura sculptures in the north, and the reliefs of Amaravati, Nagarjunakonda, etc., in the south. Besides the typical Indian costume consisting of *dhoti,* dupattas and turban for men, and sari and ordhani for women, sewn garments, such as tunics, trousers, high boots, and armor, caps, etc. probably of Central Asiatic and Iranian origin, were also worn.

Cotton cloth was extensively used. The cotton was cultivated in large plantations and there were weavers who wove fine cloths. In the south the members of the Naga tribe were proficient in the craft of weaving. The Nagas of the Kalinga country wove the finest mulsins, which were exported to foreign countries.

The Roman Empire was a great patron of Indian muslin which as exported to Rome, Egypt, Arabia, etc. from Barygaza, etc. The finest Indian muslin was known as *'ventis textiles'* or *'neubla'*. Silk was also in great demand and *pattamsuka* (plain white silk), 'china' (Chinese silk), *kauseya* (mulberr silk) and *dhautapatta* (washedsilk), were the different varieties of silk. Patola or the variegated silk *sari* of Gujarat was known as vicitrapatolaka, and the woman of South India used scarlet-flowered silk.[24]

Woolen cloth was known as dusya, several varieties of which were known. Mixed fabrics of wool and *dukula* were woven, and the beautiful shawls of Kashmir woven from the wool of the goat elicited the admiration of all. Cloths manufactured from linen, and certain fibrous fruits were also extensively used. Golden brocade under the name of *hiryani* and *hirivastra, pandukula* or cloth manufacture from the fibers of *dukula,* the silk and cotton cloth of Banares, the Aparantaka cloth of Sind, Gujara and Konkan, *phuttaka* cloth (perhaps printed calico), and *puspapatta* or 'flowered cloth' either printed or embroidered, were also known.[25]

Dhoti and *dupattas* which were sometimes of considerable value were the chief garments of the Indians. The kings wore *dhotis, dupattas,* turban and sometimes a tunic. The farmers and weaver wore a flaxen loin-cloth. Ministers, chamberlains, bankers and domestic chaplains, etc. also wore turbans. The guards at the palace gates were clad in brown tunics and armer.[26]

Tamil literature of the south it is evident that the kings wore loin-cloth, a conical crown, and ornaments. The dress of the Tamil people differed according to their status in society. The people of the middle class wore a loin-cloth and turban. The soldier guarding the king's palace wore coats. The Tamil women wore saris leaving the torso bare. Some aboriginal woman wore leaf. Literature, however, gives rather sketchy information about the customers of the people and for more detailed information we have to depend on the sculptures from various parts of India.[27]

The female costume as represented in the Gandhara sculptures consisted of these pieces, a sleeved tunic, a sort of petticoat and a shawl. The shirt generally reached to the knees and in exceptional cases opened in front: The *sari* was worn in two ways: in the first one part was wrapped round the waist and the other pleated and tucked in behind; in the second one part was wrapped round the waist and the free end thrown over the left shoulder. The *chador* was also on over the shoulders. The foreign women in the service of the king either wore classical Greek customs, tunic and *dupattas* with pleated skirts, or they wore *sari* and *chador.*[28]

The costume of the people in the *'Madhyadesa'* or middle country is depicted in the Kushana sculptures of Mathura. The indigenous costume of the men consists *of dhoti* and falling in graceful folds and *patka* or a decorative piece of cloth rucked to the *dhoti* and *kamarbands.* Turban made of rich *material* were also worn. These were invariably mounted with metallic plaeues. The Saka kings and solidiers in the Mathura sculpture generally wore a tunic, trousers, a cap and high boots. There were several varieties of tunics. The caps were generally conical in shape, though hemispherical caps are also known The women wore saris held to the waist with elaborate girdles and *dupattas*. The *kamarbands* were worn in different modes. The women of foreign origin wore a tunic and also a sari, one part of which was wrapped round the waist and the other taken over the left shoulder. The women of Mathura generally did not cover their heads though occasionally they used veils and turbans.

Fourth Century to Sixth Century A.D.

In the fourth to sixth century, the history of the decorative design in textiles and costume may be divided round under three sections: (1) pre-Gupta; (2) Gupta and (3) post-Gupta, including the period of Sri Harsa and the Calupyas of Deccdan.

The materials of costume and textile in the *Amarakosa* are of a varied nature. Various classes of textiles manufactured from bark fibers, linen, silk, wool and goat's hair are defined. Various technical terms of cloth manufacture from the loom to the washing and finishing stages are given. It also contains various terms for garments sewn or otherwise. Names for sews garments of the women, such as *cola, candataka,* etc.[31]

It is evident from the coins that the Gupta kings often wore tunics, trousers and high boots after the fashion of the Kushana kings, and very often they were also represents wearing *dhoti, dupatta,* and turban in combination with tunics and *kamarbands*. It is also evident from the coins of Kumaragupta that a national costumes was coming to the forecast in the later part of the Gupta period. The women as a rule were represented in *sari,* tunic and *chador*. The skirt was generally used by women and the common dress of Indians was a *dhoti* and *dupattas;* though in Kashmir and other colder regions sewn woolen garments were used.[32]

All the information's about Indian costume is of insignificance when we approach the, paintings of Ajanta which show us in detail the costumes of the people of all classes. It is significant that commonly the kings at Ajanta wore *dhoti* and highly ornamented head-dressed but sewn garments were not tabooed. The nobles and princes imitated the king. The chamberlain and at times the ministers wore long tunics. The soldiers wore either a *dhoti* or are clad in tunics, trousers, head scarves and high boots. The jesters and royal attendants wore tunic and boots or purely Indian costumes. The queens and the woman of higher social status wore light garments consisting of saris, skirts and scarves, though at times they also wore tunic with half sleeves or full. It was however in the costumes of the female attends that a great variety may be seen. One section of the female attends wore tunic and caps of definitely foreign origin and the other section was clad in purely Indian costume. The dancing girls were also shown wearing tunic, sometimes in combination with an apron-like garments and trousers.[33]

Eight Century to Twelfth Century A.D.

For the history of the costumes and textile materials in Northern and Western India in the eighth and ninth centuries, our chief sources are the works of the famous Jain writer Haribhadra Sun and equally famous writer and dramatist Rajasekhara (c.A.D. 880-920) in the *Kavyamimamsa* and the *Karpuramanjari* gives glimpses of the female costumes. Thus according to him the women of Bengal wore a chain necklace over breast besmeared with sandal; their *chadors* touched the partings of their hair and their forearms were exposed. The women of *Kanauj* wore earrings which moved and also the hanging tremulous necklaces. Their upper garments, falling from the thighs to the ankles, encircled the body.

In the *Karpuramanjari* more details about the garments of a lady are given. At one place *Karpuramanjari* appears with one hand arranging the border of the garment that was falling on her rounded breasts, with the other restraining the *sari*.

Twelth to Fifteenth Century

By the end of the twelth century the country was subjugated- and a hundred years later the Muslim Sultan of Delhi consolidated his owner and firmly established his supremacy over almost whole of India.

Weavers in different parts of India produced stuffs made of silks and cottons in varied textures and designs. Certain regions specialized in certain items and became renowned for them. In the South, for instanced, centers on the western and eastern coasts were known for their excellent plain and printed cottons. The kingdom of Vijaynagar produced, in addition to cottons, certain types of silks. Further north, in the Deccan, again, silks and cottons were manufactured. Among these, the muslins of Daulatabad were famous. The poet Amir Khushru speaks in superlative terms about them, claiming that 'the skin of the moon removed by the executioner star could not be so fine.' He also mentions that a hundred yards of it could pass through the eye of a needle, so fine was its texture. Elaborates upon its qualities by the comment, 'It is so transparent and light that it looks as if one is in no dress at all but has merely smeared the body with pure water.

Such delicate textiles were made also in eastern India. The muslin from Bihar according to Amir Khushru was like the pleasant gift of springtide, resting;' as lightly on the body as moonlight on the tulip or a dewdrop on the morning rose'. Further eastwards the region of Bengal excelled in the weaving of fine fabrics and silk with threads of gold.

In Kashmir, under royal patronage and encouragement, skilled craftsmen wove silks in endless threads of beautiful colours and intricate designs. They also mastered the art of making embroidered carpets and produced stuffs comparable to those brought 'from distant lands and worthy of king's.[36]

The provinces of Gujarat too, was extremely productive with many centers busily engaged in the manufacture of textiles. Gujarat, moreover, served as the hub of the textile trade, a place where stuffs from different parts of India were brought and tunneled into the export market.

The extensive manufacture and trade in textiles resulted in the availability of indigenous and foreign fabrics of diferent types and textures. The *Darul Adi* market, recounts Amir Khushru, contained all kinds of cloth from cotton to silks which hide the body, from Bihar Muslim to lowered *jamandi* silk used both in summer and in winter, from tapestry, woven carpet which greatly differs in their fibers and from silk to plush velvet made from silk and wool which are similar in their structures and from Daulatabad Muslim which are allurement for mind and body'. As many as 200 varieties of cloth-existed in those das judging from the contemporary Hindu, Muslim and Portuguese writings as well as the stocks lists maintained by the Gujarat merchants.[37]

The names of the fabrics too, provide interesting information such as silk from Gujarat and Tanjore silk indicate their place of manufacture while others like silk comparable to the inside of a banana tree-trunk and silk with luster of pearls suggest texture. Some words like the striped silk and cloth with geese motif, describe the pattern and some like five-colour silk and pigeon-coloured silk are evocative of colour.

Indian materials were often combined with foreign ones to make robes for the kings and their wives, as also robes of honor for presentation to amirs.

Materials of deluxe quality such as foreign fabrics, embroidered brocades, indigenous silks and fine muslins could never be used by the common people; such stuffs were the prerogative of people of rank and those upon whom the Sultan conferred the privilege. Occasionally articles of wear made for the Hindu and Muslim aristocracy were enriched further with decorations in gold thread and jewels.[39]

Thirteenth Century School of Western Indian Painting

Men had long hair, usually tied in a knot at the nape of the neck, and long beards. They dressed in a short *dhoti* or light-fitting shorts and an *uttariya* draped around the hips and transversely across the end over the shoulder. When the *uttariya* was held in the hands it signified. The sleeved-jacket, a common item to wear in the preceding century appeared infrequently. The men did not wear anything on their feet. Their garments consisted of a tiara, ear-rings, necklaces, armlets, bracelets and anklets.

Fourteenth and Fifteenth Centuries—Gujarat and Rajasthan

Kings and Courtiers often supported a short beard or moustache and their long hair were tied in a knot at the back of the head. They wore a *dhoti,* and an *uttariya* made of fine materials. The *uttariya* was draped around the hips, diagonally across the chest, over the shoulder and across the back. It was then left hanging loosely at the back. They were without footwear. For ornaments they used a tiara, hair ornaments which sometimes included a jewelled fillet to keep the knotted hair in place, ear-rings, necklaces, armlets, bracelets and anklets. They also wore a U-shaped *tilak mark* on the forehead.

Commoners dressed similarly, not donning the tiara but a cap or a cloth handkerchief tied around the hair-knot and with much fewer ornaments. Musicians were dressed in the same manner as the commoners. Warriors, generally, did not dress differently from other men except that they often replaced their tiara with a cap or a small scarf tied around their knotted hair so as to keep it in place. They carried a sword and a shield. On occasion they wore trousers with high boots, herds wore a *dhoti* and *uttariya* and a cap-like head-geat.[42]

Jain Monks and Nuns dressed as in the preceding period except that the fabrics they used were finer in quality and often employ a self-design in the weave. Women wore their hair in a deed plait or a knot placed either at the nape or high at the back of the head. Their outfit consisted of three pieces: a *dhoti,* a *choli* with elbow-length sleeves and an *odhani-* one end of which was draped around the hips, across the chest over the shoulder and across the back. It was left hanging at the back. The women did not wear anything on their feet. They adorned themselves with a tiara, hair ornaments including a jewelled comb aobe the plait or the hair-knot, three types of ear-rings, one at the top, one in the middle and one in the ear several necklaces of varying lengths, bracelets and ankelets. They put a *Bindi* on the forehead. This style of women's dress closely parallels that of the Gujarat women of the sixteenth century whom *Duarte Barbosa* described as being clad in 'dresses as long as their husband's; they wore silken bodices with tight sleeves, cut low at the back and other long garments called, *chador,* which they throw over themselves like cloaks.

Sahi Kings and Courtiers, probably of central Asian origin, where bearded and with their hair tied in a long tasseled plait. Over a long-sleeved white shirt made of fine cotton or silk they wore a long heavy gown of brocade or velvet. The gown had short sleeves and gold embroidery along the collar and the sleeves. A variation of this basic type was visible in a robe with overlapping flaps wrapped around the body and held at the waist by a cloth belt. A heavy collar, either of separate metal piece or intricately embroidered in gold, a metal belt and knee-high boots completed the outfit. The dress of the *Sahi* Kings matched, to a fair extent, the Muslim aristocracy, they wore gowns which at times had gold embroidered sleeves and occasionally gold embroider between the shoulders, their head-dress was four corner in shape and ornamented with jewels; they plaited their hair in hanging locks with silk tassels; their waists were encircled with gold and silver belts and they wore shoes and *Sahi* Soldiers were attained in a short tunic with overlapping flaps and tight-fitting trousers. Other articles of dress consisted of a headed gear in the form of a turban, belt shin-guards, and shoes. They carried a sword and a shield.[44]

Fifteenth Century Delhi and Gwalior

Men, sometimes bearded, wore their long hair twisted and bound in a multi-tiered knot high at the back of their head. Most of them dressed in the short rather than the long *dhoti*. It was worn with the pleats projecting forward or passed backwards through the legs. Sometimes a sash was wound around the waist and its loosely hanging end was worn in the same manner as the *dhoti* pleats. The *uttariya* was draped around the hips and taken transversely across the chest and over the shoulder or left to hanging downwards from the neck and over the shoulders. Once in a while a tight, sleeved jacket upto the waist was worn. As in Western India, people went barefooted. The jewellery consisted of a high tiara, ear-rings, necklaces, armlets, bracelets and anklets. Warriors attired themselves in the same clothes as worn by other men except that they were armed with a sword or bow and arrows and a shield. Tribal Men wore a short skirt and a head-dress. The Chief of the tribe wore a feathered headdress. *Shaivite* Sage is seen in a loose striped tunic.

Women wore their hair in a knot just above the neck and dressed in a *dhoti, bandi* upto the waist with elbow-length sleeves and a *odhani,* one end of which was round around the hips taken the chest over the shoulder and allowed the head and the two ends hung loosely at the back, or it was not worn at all. The women adorned themselves in either a high tiara or a small jewel on the forehead in the parting of the hair, hair ornaments, ear rings, heavy necklaces armlets, brackets and anklets.[45]

The Indian male now adopted *the jama,* and article to wear of the Muslim gentry, in his attire the *jama* was of different types, either a short one with a *pajama* or a long one reaching the ankles. Sometimes *the jama* was replaced by a single piece of clothing consisting of a tunic with *pajamas. The jama* took the form of a gown or a robe with overlapping flaps and was held at the waist by a belt or a *patka.* At first this item of dress was adopted for certain occasions like expeditions of war or the hunt but then, gradually, it becomes part of the regular attire.

In the female attire the *sari* was introduced. It was worn with a *choli,* pleated in the front and the loose end passed over the head and across the breasts to flare out on the side. The high tiaras of the earlier period gave way to low ones.[46] The fabrics portrayed in the painting of this region appeared to be coarse in texture and rudimentary in design. The materials were other plain in colour or patterned in stripes or simple motifs like dots and crosses. No where do we encounter the fine fabrics with exquisite design as in the painting of western India. Both types of textiles, without doubt, reflect the stuffs commonly employed in the two regions.[47]

Fourteenth and Fifteenth Century—Mughal Costumes

The transition of the court culture from the Sultanates to the Mughals was not as abrupt as may seem from the struggle for power between them. The Pathans, who had begun to infiltrate after Qutb-ud-Din Aibak' victory and settlement at Mehrauli, shared their language and way of life with the Persians, by virtue of the fact that large parts of Iran and Afghanistan were part of the Khorasan kingdom of Tamur's descendants.

The Sultans retained the Persian gown like tunic for winter wear, with baggy *salwars* for the lower part the body, but they preferred clothes made from brocade for the winters and Muslim for the summers, varied by costumes made from cotton and wool for in-between seasons. The gentle women kept the long gown, like the *Makati* robe of Baghdad, only embroidered with gold, with *salwars* underneath. The bulk of the population retained the traditional intertwining of the two sheets, in the plain white for; men and in dyed and printed cloths for women, especially for the *ghagra,* skirt, and the *dupatta.*[48]

Under Babur and Humayun, the first two Mughals, there was a rough and ready adaptation of the *Uzbek tunic,* trousers and long boots of the soldiery to lighter weight costumes. Akbar's sense of glory inspired everything. The dynamic young Emperior, who had by his perceptive genuis, seen that only the synthesis of the conquering Uzbek way of life with the styles of living of the natives, would make for a stable empire, deliberately married Jodhabai, the daughter of Raja Bihari Mal of Jaipur and adopted many of the customs of his chief queen's household. In clothes, Akbar encouraged the *chokidar jama* with six pointed lapel ends below the gown-like cloak in various colours, yellow, orange, purple. This was probably been adopted from Rajasthan, where the style of cloak was current as evidenced in the Chaurapanchashika paintings of western India. Also he adapted the readymade tied turbans of the Rajputs, which looked like a crown, when the nobles had precious stones put in tiaras on it. The *patka,* belt which secured the waist, was like in brocade, with square and crosses printed on it. The *pajama* was nearly *churidar,* also perhaps taken from Rajasthani courts. The shoes were horn-shaped at the back and embroidered with zari work. A gold chain held the dagger roosted to *the patka.* This was court dress for winter.[49]

In the summers the nobles wore the same style of clothes, in muslin or other light material, with the *churidan pajama* in cotton cloth. The ladies of the nobility adopted the colourful *ghagra* of Rajasthan, the *choli* which shaped the breasts and the *odhani* in diaphanous silks, muslims and woolen shawls. The women servants of the *zenana* wore the same style of clothes as the noblewomen, only in rougher materials. There were fewer pom-poms and tassels on their dresses.

In Jehangir's time, the costume became more opulent. The Emperor himself set the fashion for decorating the Akbaride turban, with pearls and plumes of rare bires. Only the princes adorned themselves with the head-dress. The nobles continued to wear the tied turban, more or less plain, though in one colour or the other. The cloak of silk was now no longer with pointed ends below, and it was in pastel shade of silks, or in broacade. The *churidar pajama* was in soft green silk. The horns at the back of the shoes disappeared and gave place to leisurely slippers made of red leather. *The patka* was often a kind of scrawl printed with foliage, on blue or pink background. The sash was of gold cloth, with geometric designs, insert with pastel shade flowers. The main styles can be traced back to Rajasthan and Gujarat, where the weaving of cloth and dyeing and printing had been practiced for centuries with utmost taste worships for supplies of cloth to the Agra court were not only in the capital, but in the villages around, and in the nearby old provincial centers. Several lakhs of weavers, dyes and printers were busy providing for the nobles and their wives.

In Shahjehan's time, the love of rich and colourful costumes got a further fillip from the extravagant Emperor. It was known that Shahjehan was a connoisseur of brocades and jewellery and had workshops established specially for the craftsmen near Chandni Chowk in Delhi, when he had built the Red Fort in Shahjehanabad. The nobles took the fashions of the court to the various provinces when they were sent on duty in outlying areas.[52]

Aurangzeb expressly forbade the wearing of pure silk at court. Himself, he retained the style of cloak and turban of his father, on made in coarser cloth. On state occasions, he adorned himself with jewellery, including necklaces, pendent, bracelets, and a dagger with a handle of jade. He preferred the colour green as an orthodox Muslim.[53]

Fifteenth to Seventeeth Century Decani's Costumes

The costumes of the prince and noblemen were modeled on the clothes which were familiar in the time of Amir Khusro. The import of silks called *Khaz, Aksun* and *Parniyan* continued from Cathay as well as from West Asian. These silks were embroidered with gold preferred in the south, because of warm climate nine months in the year. These silks were so fine, that a hundred yards could be easily passed through the eye of a needle, as the ornamental phrase has it. The style of the twelth, thirteen and fourteen centuries in the Deccan did not differ much from the North. But the emergence of the Vijaynagar Empire, the Hindu costume especially of women, began to influence, the fashion of the *Zenanas* of the sultans, also the rich fabric women in Vijaynagar began to be popular, because of the legendary splendor attached to everything made there. A copper plate of A.D. 1382 of Vijaynagar, mentions the use of rich wedding cloths, white cloth, silk cloth, raw silks, spun cotton, woolen stuffs, sack cloth, and shawls. From the Deccani paintings of the medieval period, certain unique fashions of original design are visible. The upper garment for men, though remaining the *chakdar jama* of pointed lower ends, has four to six hanging points on the torso. The patka was highly decorative and the sash was often embroidered with gold.[55]

The noble women wore a three-piece garment. A *sari* draped as a skirt, a choli covering the torso, though open at the back and an almost transparent *odhani* with soft slippers on the feet The decorative pom-poms, tassels and sashes heighten the wrists, the shoulders, the pigtails and the girdle. The *odhani* is mostly of transparent muslin, often with polka dots in groups of three. The *colours* purple and mauve are preferred. An apron-like patka hangs down in lyrical lines from the front of the waist. The fusion of the costumes of Hindus and Muslims was achieved in some of the *zenanas* of the Southern Sultans, especially when they married hindu women.[56]

Costume has been functioning as a fashioner of personality and has tended to be cultivated as an art in today's world. As every community has its unique way of dressing which at a glance distinguish it from the others communities for example Rajasthani women wear *Odhni, ghaghra* and *Choli,* while Punjabi women wear *Salwar, Kurta* and *Dupatta*. Similarly every tribe has its unique costume which distinguish it from other tribal groups.

With the passage of time and as new invention emerge in the horizon, changes are seen in all the phases of life. The effect of changing devices on Tribal society could not be saved, they have also join steadily the main stream of national life. Now we can see the effect of changing face in the tribal culture, in the vaster of culture matrix, some of the elements are still remain encountered, one most significant element among this is costume which is one of the three basic needs of human being i.e. food, clothing and shelter. The details of the garments and ornaments such as fabrics, designs, pattern of garments, metal used in jewellery, weight of the ornament, designs of the ornament, motifs of tattooing, etc. are still not known.

REFERENCES

1. John Carl Flugel, (1930), The Psychology of Clothes, Hogarth Press & the Institute of Psychoanalysis, p. 86.
2. *Ibid.*, p. 108.
3. E. Adamson Hobel, Man in the Primitive World: An inroduction to Anthropology (2nd ed.: New York: MC Grow-Hill Book Co. 1958), pp. 248-49.
4. *Ibid.*, p. 241.
5. *Ibid.*, p. 241
6. Edmund Bergler, Fashion and the inconcious (New york: Robert Burnner, 1953), p. 26.
7. Flugel, p. 26
8. James Laver, “Laver’s Law” interview, Women’s wear Daily, July 13, 1964, pp. 4-5.
9. Havelock Ellis, Studies in the Psychology of sex IV: The Evolution of Modesty, Vol. I. (New York: Random House, Inc. 1942), p. 172.
10. Bernard Roshco, The Bag Race (New York: Fank and Wagnalls, Inc. 1963), p. 138
11. Flugel, pp. 108-109.
12. *Ibid.*, p. 185
13. *Ibid.*, p. 188

14. C. Willett Cunnington, why women wear clother (London: Faber & Faber Ltd., 1941), p. 42.
15. J. Marshall, Monhenjo-daro and the Indus Civilisation, London, (1931), Vol. III, p. 18.
16. *Ibid.*, p. 21.
17. Bhatnagar Parul Traditional Indian Costumes and Textiles, Chandigarh, Abishekh Publication, (2003), p. 104.
18. Kay, Talwarand Kalyan Krishna, Indian Pigement Painting on Cloth, Ahmedabad, (1979), p. 25.
19. *Ibid.*, p. 32.
20. Alkargi, Roshan, Ancient Indian Costumes, (1983). An Heritage Books Publication p. 57-59.
21. Baden-Powell, Handbook of the manufacturers and Arts of the Punjab, Lahore, (1872), p. 09.
22. Janet Harry, Traditional Textiles of Central Asia, (1978), p. 12.
23. Gejur, Agnes, A History of Textile Art, (1979), p. 104.
24. *Ibid.*, p. 106.
25. *Ibid.*, p. 127.
26. *Ibid.*, p. 130.
27. *Ibid.*, p. 136.
28. Chandra, Moti, "Costumes, Textiles, Cosmetics & Coiffure in Ancient & Mediaeval India, Delhi, (1973), pp. 47.
29. *Ibid.*, p. 51.
30. *Ibid.*, p. 102.
31. *Ibid.*, p. 114.
32. *Ibid.*, p. 117.
33. Bhavani Enakshi, "Folk and Tribal Designs of India", Taraparewala, Mumbai (1974), p. 92.
34. Chandra, Moti "Prachin Bhartiya Vesha Bhusha Mumbai, (1950), p. 42.
35. *Ibid.*, p. 56.
36. *Ibid.*, p. 74.
37. *Ibid.*, p. 91.
38. *Ibid.*, p. 93.
39. *Ibid.*, p. 98.
40. MARG, XV, 4, Traditional Textiles of India, (1962), p. 83.

41. *Ibid.*, p. 94.
42. *Ibid.*, p. 95.
43. *Ibid.*, p. 97.
44. *Ibid.*, p. 104.
45. Kramresicha, Stella, 'Kantha', Journal of Indian Society of Oriental Art, VII (1993), p. 72.
46. *Ibid.*, p. 83.
47. *Ibid.*, p. 84.
48. Karen, Baclawshi, "Agude to historic Costume, (1948), p. 89
49. *Ibid.*, p. 114.
50. *Ibid.*, p. 116.
51. Kamla S. Dongerkery, "The Romance of Indian Embroidery" (1951), p. 63.
52. *Ibid.*, p. 82.
53. *Ibid.*, p. 102.
54. Agarwal, V.S. "References to Textiles in "Banana's Harshacharita, Journal of Indian Textile History, (1959), p. 27.
55. *Ibid.*, p. 31.
56. *Ibid.*, p. 33.

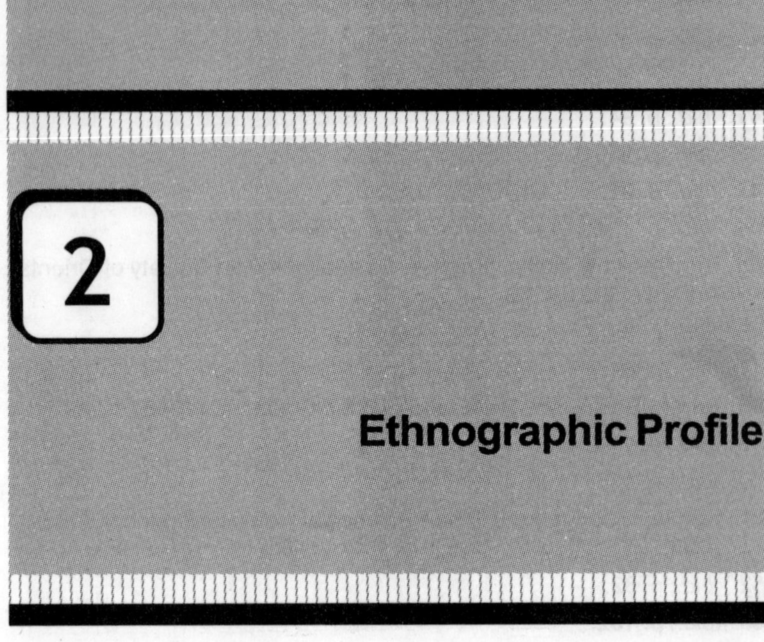

2

Ethnographic Profile

BHILS

The name Bhil is derived from the Dravidian word for a bow, which is the characteristic weapon of the tribe, and by others from the root of the Sanskrit word meaning "to pierce, shoot or kill (Bhedna)", in consequence of their proficiency as archers.

Origin

There are numberous legends regarding the origin of these people. According to one, Mahadeo, sick and unhappy, was reclining in a shady forests when there appeared before him a beautiful woman, the first sight of whom effected a complete cure of all his ailments. An intercourse between the god and the strange female was established, the result of which was many children; one of the latter, who was from infancy distinguished alike by his ugliness and vice, slew his father's favrout bull and for this crime he was expelled to the woods and mountains, and his descendants have ever since been stigmatised with the names of Bhil and Nishada, terms that denote outcastes.[1] Another version is that the first Bhil was created by Mahadeo by breathing life into a doll of clay; while the *Bhagavat Puran* says that the tribe is descended from a mythical *Raja* called Vena, the son of Anga, who ruled his people with a rod of iron, compelled them to worship him, prohibited the performance of *yajna* and other religious ceremonies, and generally so exasperated the *Rishis* (sages) that they killed him by *mantras* (incantations).[2] There being no one to succeed him as ruler, the country became greatly disturbed and, to restore order, the *Rishis begat* from Vena's dead body a dwarfish person who came to be known as *Nishada;* he is described as being in colour as dark as the crow; his limbs were too small, his cheek-bones prominent, his nose flat, and his eyes blood-red, and his descendants lived in the mountains.and jungles.

The Bhil seen to be *Pygmies* of Otesias 1400 B.C.), who described them as black and ugly, the tallest being only two evil high, their hair and beards were so long that they served as garments, and they were excellent bowmen and very honest. In the Adi Parva of the Mahabharata, mention is made of a *Nishada* or Bhil, Eklavya, who had acquired great mastery over the bow by practicing before the clay image of Dronacharya, the tutor of the Pandavas, and who, on the request of Arjuna, one of the five brothers, unhestitatingly cut off his right thumb and presented it to him as a *dakshina* (fee). The tribe has also been identified with the Poulindai and Phyllitoe of Ptolemy (150 A.D.), but the name by which they are at present known cannot be traced far back in *Sanskrit* literature, the term *"Bhilla"* seeming to occur for the first time about 600 A.D.[3]

Early Habitations

The Bhils are among the oldest inhabitants of the country and are said to have entered India from the north and north-east several hundred years before the Christrian era, and to have been driven to their present fastnesses at the time of the Hindu invasion. Colonel Tod, however, seems to scout the idea of their having come from a distance; he calls them *Vanaputras* or children of the forest, "the uncultivated mushrooms of India, fixed, as the rocks and trees of their mountain wilds, to the spot which gave them birth.[4] This entire want of the organ of locomotion, and unconquerable indolence of character which seems to possess no portion of that hardiness which can brave the dangers of migration, forbid all idea of their foreign origin and would rather incline us to the Monboddo theory that they are an improvement of the tribe with tails. They do not recall that their raids from their jungle-abodes in search of plunder supply any argument against the innate principle of locality. The Bhil returns to it as truly as does the needle to the north; nor could the idea enter his mind of seeking other regions for a domicile".[5]

So far, however, as Rajputana is concerned, it may be asserted that, prior to the Rajput conquest, the tribe held a great deal of the southern half of the Province. The annals of Mewar, for example, frequently mention the assistance rendered by the Bhils to the early Gahlot rulers; the towns of Dungarpur, Banswara, and Deolia (the old capital of Partabgarh) are all named after some Bhil chieftain who for merely held away there; and the country in the vicinity of Kota city was wrested by a chief a Bundi from a community of Bhils called Koteah. Lastely, it is well known that in three States, (Udaipur, Banswar and Dungarpur), it was formerly the custom, when a new chief succeeded to the *gaddi,* to mark his bow with blood taken from the thumb or toe of a Bhil of a particular family.[6] The Rajputs considered the blood-mark to a sign of Bhil allegiance, but it seems to have been rather a relic of Bhil power.[7] The Bhils were very persistent in keeping alive the practice, and the popular belief that the man from whose veins the blood was taken would die within a year failed to damp their zeal; the Rajputs on the other hand, were anxious to let the practice die out as they shrank, they said, from the application of the impure Bhil blood, but the true ground of their dislike to the ceremony was probably due to the acknowledgement which it conveyed of their need of investiture by an older and conquered race.[8] In Udaipur the right of giving the blood was originally accorded to a family living at Oghna in the Hilly Tracts, in recognition of services rendered to Bapa Rawal in the eighth century, and is said to have been enjoyed by it till the time of Rana Hamir Singh in the fourteenth century, when the custom ceased. In Dungarpur the Balwaia sept possessed the right, and is believed to have exercised it till fairly recent times.

Clans

The tribe is sub-divided into a large number of clans, some based on reputed common descent, and others Apparently hurddled together as a group by simple contiguity of habitation or by the banding together of neighbours for plunder or self-defence; the members of each sub division reside for the most part in separate *pals* or villages and do not intermarry. From the Hilly Tracts or Mewar sixteen distinct clans have been reported, from Dungarpur twenty-six, from Partabgarh thirty-seven, and from Jodhpur fifty-eight.[9] Some call themselves *ujla* or pure Bhils, but they are few in number; they are supposed not to eat anything white in colour, such as a white sheep or goat, and their grand adjuration is "By the white ram" Others claim descent from almost every clan of Rajput and prefix the name thereof, e.g. *Bhati, Chauhan, Gahlot, Makwana, Paramara, Rathor* and *Solanki*. Each clan, indeed each village, has its leader or headman, usually termed *gameti*.

Three Main Classes

The Bhils have, by the various changes in their condition, been divided into three classes which may be denominated the village, the cultivating, and the wild or mountain Bhil.[10] The first consists of those who, from ancient residence or change, have become inhabitants of villages in the plain (though usually near the hills), of which they are the watchman and are incorporated as a portion of the community. The cultivating Bhils are those who have continued in their peaceable occupations after their leaders were destroyed or driven by invaders to become desperate free-boosters. Specimens of these two classes are to be found in almost every State. The third class, that of the wild or mountain Bhil, comprises all that part of the tribe which preferring savage freedom and indolence to submission and industry, has continued more or less to subsistant by plunder, and its home is the south of Rajputana. Each group alternately decreases or increases in number according to the fluctuations in the neighbouring governments, when these have been strong and prosperous, the village and cultivating Bhils have drawn recruits from their wilder brethren, while weakness, confusion and oppression have had the usual effect of driving the industrious of the tribe to desperate courses; but abide all changes, there is ever a disposition in each branch of the community to reunite, and this is derived from their preserving the same usages and the same form of religion."

Occupations in the Past

The Bhils, as a whole, have always been lawless and independent, fond of fighting, shy, excitable and restless. Believing themselves doomed to be thieves and plunderers, they were confirmed in their destiny by the oppression and cruelty of their rulers. The common answer of a Bhil, when charged with robbery, was "I am not to blame, I am Mahadeo's thief."[12] The Marathas treated them like wild animals and ruthlessly killed them whenever encountered; if caught red-handed committing serious crimes, they were impaled on the spot or burnt to death, chained to a red-hot iron seat. About the time of our treaties with the Rajput chiefs, the wilder Bhils in the Mewar Hilly Tracts and Bansawara and Dungarpur gave much trouble by their claim to leave blackmail throughout their country and their inveterate habits of plundering. It was difficult either to pursue them into their fastnesses or to fix the responsibility on the State to which they belonged territorially, expeditions sent under British officers against them rarely effected anything permanent, while the Darbars were only strong enough to oppess and exasperate them, without subduing them.

Reclamation

Since the intervention of the British Government about 1824, followed some sixteen years later by the establishment of the Mewar Bhil Crops, these people have been treated with kindness and are now fairly pacified; the measures by which they were gradually reaimed from some of the most honourable episodes of Anglo-Indian rule.[14] In the Mutiny of 1857 the only native troops in Rajputant that stood by their British officers were the Mewara Battalion (now the 44th Mewara Infantry), the Bhil companies of the Erinpura Irregular Force (now the 43rd Erinpura Regiment), and the Mewar Bhils Groups; service in the latter has for many years been so popular that the supply of recruits always exceeds the demand. It must not be supposed that the Bhils have altogether given up their predatory and quarrelsome habits; they still lift cattle and abduct women, and these actions give rise to retaliatorty affrays which are occasionally serious. In times of famine and scarcity, or when their feelings have been aroused by some injudicious act on the part of their ruler, they are also still inclined to take the law into their own hands, but the bad characters and professional robbers are now distinctly in the minority. Many are peaceful, if unskillful and indolent, cultivators, and earn a respectable livelihood as such, or by cutting and selling grass, manufacturing rude baskets, cleaning cotton, or serving as *shikaris,* guides, and messengers. The Mewar Bhil Corpus contains a body of loyal and obedient soldiers, and the pensioners of the corps have, by their influence, done much to keep their wild brethren in order.[15]

Characteristics

Some of the characteristics* of the tribe have already been mentioned, such as lawlessness, independence, shyness, etc; to these we may add truthfulness, hospitality, obedience to recognized authority, and confidence and respect for the *Sarkar* (the British Government). As regards truthfulness, it is said that those who live in the wilder and more inaccessible parts never lie, while those who have come into contact with the civilization of towns and larger villages soon lose this ancient virtue.

If, however, a Bhil pledges protections, he will sacrifice his life to redeem his word; the travellers through his passes has but to pay the customary tool, and his property and person are secure, and any insult or injury by another will be avenged. The Bhil's obedience to recognized authority is absolute, and Tod relates how the wife of an absent chieftain procured for a British messenger safe conduct and hospitality through the densest forests by giving him one of her husband's arrow as a token. The same writer tells us that in the conflicts between the Ranas of Mewar and the emperor of Delhi, "the former were indebted to these children of the forest for their own preservation and, what is yet more dear to a Rajput, that of their wives and daughters from the hands of a foe whose touch was pollution". Again in more recent times when Udaipur city was besieged by Sindhia, "its protacted defence was in a great measure due to the Bhils who conveyed supplies to the besieged across the lake".

The principal failing of the tribe is an inordinate thirst for liquor, which is very much an evidence of all occasion such as births, betrothals, marriages, deaths, festivals and *panchayats.*

---

*About thirty years ago, a native student in an examination for a University degree described the tribe thus: The Bhil is a very black man, but more hairy. He carries in his hand a long spear, with which he runs you when he meets you, and afterwards throws your body into the ditch. By this you may know the Bhil.

Their quarrels begin and end in drunken bouts; no feud can be stached, no crime forgiven but at a general feat. The common and popular fine for every offence is more liquor to protact their riotous enjoyment which sometimes continues for days.

The woman are said to have considerable influence in the society, and in olden days were noted for their humane treatment of such prisoners as their husbands ami relatives brought in, they are generally very particular in their relations with the opposite sex after marriage, but not so usually before. The fine for the seduction of a virgin is about Rs. 60 which is given to her parents, and the man is compelled to marry the girls. Such cases are always adjudicated by a *panchayat*.

Superstitions

The Bhils are very superstitious, and wear charms and amulets on the right forearm to keep ghosts and spirits at a distance. They also religiously believe in witchcraft, and there are *bhopas* or witch-finders in many of the large villages, whose duty it is to point out the woman who has caused the injury. Before a woman is swung as a witch, she is compelled to undergo some sort of ordeal, the primitive judge's method of referring difficult cases to a higher court for decision.[16] The orderal by water is most common. Sometimes the woman is placed in one side of a bullock's pack-sack and three dry cakes of cow-dung in the other; the sack is then thrown into the water, and if the woman sink, she is no witch, while if she swim, she is. Here is a description of a water test taken not many years ago from the mouth of an expert *bhopa* who got into trouble for applying it to an old woman. "A bamboo is stuck up in the middle of any piece of water. The accused is taken to it, lays hold of it, and by it descends to the bottom. In the meantime one of the villagers shoots and arrow from his bow, and another runs to pick it up and bring it back to the place when it was shot. If the woman is able to remain under water until this is done, she is declared innocent; but it she comes up to breathe before the arrow is returned into the woman's hand, she is a true witch and must be swung as such".[17] In the case from which this account is taken, the woman failed in the test and was accordingly swang to and fro, roped up to a tree, with a bandage of red pepper on her eyes.

It is obvious, however, that this kind of ordeal, like almost all primitive modes of trial, is contrived so as to depend for its effect much upon the manner in which it is conducted whereby the operator's favour becomes worth gaining. A skilful archer will shoot just as far as he chooses, and the man who runs to recover the arrow can select his own pace.

Another form of trial is by sewing the suspected one in a sack which is left down into water about three feet deep. If the person inside the sack can get her head above water, she is a witch. An English officer once saved a woman from duckirig to death by insisting that the witch-finder and the accusers generally should go through precisely the same or deal which they had prescribed. This idea hit off the crowd's notion of fair play, and the trial was adjourned since die by consent.[18] Another ordeal is by heat as, for instance, the picking of a coin out of burning oil; but the question extraordinary is by swinging on a sacred tree or by flogging with switches of a particular wood. The swinging is done head downwards from a bough and continues till the victim confesses or dies; if she confesses, she is taken down and either killed with arrow or turned out of the villages. In 1865 a woman suspected of bringing cholera into a village was deliberately beaten to death with rods of the castrol-oil tree, which is said to be excellent for purging witchcraft. It is not unusual to knock out the front teeth of a notorous witch, the practice being seemingly connected with the belief that witches assume animal shapes.[19]

Cases of witch-swinging are nowadays rare, out a bad one was reported from Banswara three years ago. A Bhil's son being ill, a *bhopa* was consulted as to the cause, and he accused two women, both Bhil widows. They were swung up and, though both protested innocence, were beaten on the buttocks, thighs and breasts with a burning stick, liquor was put in their mouths and red pepper in their eyes. One of them died within a few hours, but the other, who had been less severely treated, was alive when cut down and eventually survived. The accuser and witch-finder were transported for life.[20]

Omen are also believed in, for instance, a cat crossing a Bhil's path when starting on any particular business will send him home again at once; if the *devi* or black sparrow chirp on the left when going out and on the right at reaching the destination, sure success will attend the undertaking. Again, the owl hooting from the same directions and positions as the *devi* augurs good luck; and similarly, if the *malare* or the *bharvi* (other kinds of sparrows) chirp on the right a: starting and on the left at reaching the destination, the traveler is considered every fortunate. But the chirping or hooting, as the case may be, of these birds, if contrary to what is deemed auspicious, forebodes certain calamity.

Habitations

The majority of the Bhils confine themselves to the wilder portions of the country, and live in *pals* or collections of detached huts amongst the hills, each hut standing on a small knoll in the midst of its patch of cultivated land. The *pals,* which consist sometimes of several hundred huts, cover an immense area and are generally divided into a number of *paras* or *phalas* (hamlets). The various huts are at some distance from each other, and this mode of living, by preventing surprise, gives these wild people greater security. The jungle on the larger hills in the vicinity is allowed to grow so that, in case of attack, they with their families and cattle can fly to it for cover. Each homestead is complete in itself, consisting of a few huts for the accommodation of cattle or the storage of grain in addition to that used for dwelling purposes, all within a single enclosure. The Bhils make their own houses, the walls being either of mud and stones or bamboos or wattle and daub, while the roofs are now usually of clay tiles, though sometimes of straw and leaves, and in shape like a beehive. The interior is kept neat and clean, and the furniture consists of one or two bedsteads interwoven with bamboo bark, some utensil made generally of clay but rarely of metal, a millstone for grinding corn, and a bamboo cradle.[21]

Food

Tod writes that the Bhils stomach "would not revolt at an offal-feeding jackal, a hideous gauna or half-putrid kine", and this might be the case even at the present day if the Bhil were actually starving, but not under ordinary circumstances. The tribe is doubtless not to very particular as to its food, but there are reported to be certain things which it will not touch, e.g. the flesh of the dog, the Bhil constant companion in the chase; or of the monkey (universally worshipped in the form of Hanuman) or of the alligator, lizard, rat or snake. The ordinary food of the people is maize or jowar, or the inferior millets, and the products of the forest; they sometimes eat rice and on festive occasions the flesh of the buffalo or goat. They are without exception fond of tobacco and, as already stated, much addicted to liquor, which is distilled from the flowers of the *mahua* tree *(Bassia latifolia)* or from the bark of the *babul (Acacia arabica)* or from molasses.

Language

The Bhil languages are imperfectly known, but belong to the Aryan family, being intermediate between Hindi and Gujarati, though they have many peculiar words. Their songs are neither very intelligible more melodious, when the Marwari proverb :- *Kain Charan ri chakri, kain arun ri rakh, kain Bhil ro gaono, kain Sathia ri sakh,* which means: Service under a Charan, the ashes of the arun wood, the songs of the Bhils, and the evidence of Sathia (a low caste) are of little consequence.[22]

Education

Education is practically non-existent, but there are a few school in Udaipur and Dungarpur at which Bhil children attend, and the recruits of the Mewar Bhil Corps are sent to the regimental school. The last census report does not give the number of literate Bhils, but tells us that only 340 Animists (307 males and 33 females) were able to read and write, and that one of them knew English. As more than ninety-one per cent of the Animists were Bhils and the remainder consisted mostly of tye wilder section of the Minas and the equally backward as Garasias, it may be said that in 1901, among the Bhils, sixteen in every 10,000 of the males and two in every 10,000 of the females were literate.[23]

Religion

The tribe returned as Animists and the rest as Hundus; the latter belonged to the village or cultivating classes, and were found only in Bikaner, Bundi, Jaipur Jhalawar, Kishangarh, Shahpura and Tonk. For census purposes as Animist was one who was not locally acknowledged as either a Hindu, Musalman, Jain, Parsi, Christian, or Buddhist, but the process of hinduism has been so long in progress that the distinction between the tribal forms of faith and the lower developments of Hinduism is very faith. The religion of the wild or mountain Bhil may be said to be a mixture of Animism and Hinduism. The former term has already been defined (page 37-38 *supra)* while the latter has been described as "Animism more or less transformed by philosophy" or as "magic tempered by metaphysics". Hinduism comprises two entirely different sets of ideas; at the one and lower end is Animism, which "seeks by means of magic to ward off or to forestall physical disasters, which looks no further than the world of sense and seeks to make that as tolerable as the conditions will permit", and at the other end is Pantheism, i.e. "the doctrine that all the countless deities and all the great forces and operations of nature, such as the wind, the rivers, the earthquakes and the pestilences, are merely direct manifestations of the pervading divine energy which shows itself in numberless forms and manners".

Thus, while the Bhils have some dim notations of the existence of a divine being and believe to a certain extent in the transmigration of souls, especially of wicked souls, they are convinced that ghosts wander about and that the spirits of the dead haunt the places occupied by them in their lifetime and will do them harm unless propitiated. The usual symbols of worship are cairns erected on the tops of hills and platforms on which stand blocks of stone smeared with red paint. The cairns are piles of loose stones on which they place rude images of a horses, burn small lamps in fulfillment of vows, and usually hand pieces of cloth; the effigies of the horse have a hole through which the spirits of the deceased are supposed to enter, and travel up to paradise, and on arrival there are animal is made over to propitiate the local deity and swell his train of warhorses. Goats and male buffaloes are sometimes sacrificed as propitiatory offerings to *Mata,* the flesh being eaten by the worshippers after that goddess is supposed to be satisfied. Their favourite deities in addition to Mata, are Mahadeo and his consort Parbati, Hanuman and Bhairon; in the Hilly Tracts of Mewar and in Dungarpur many of them have great faith in the idol at the famous Jain shrine of Rakhabh Dev and call the god *Kalaji Bapji* from the colour of the image there. Another popular local deity in Udaipur is Khagaldeo, probably a form of snake worship, while in parts of Jodhpur the Bhils show much respect to Pabu, (a hero who is said to have performed prodigies of valour and is represented in many temples as riding on a horse with a spear in his hand), and to the Kabirpanthi Sadhus.[25]

Priesthood

The Bhils, having no priests of their own, sometimes employ Brahnians, but usually resort to the *gurus* of the Chamars, *Balais* and *Bhambis* who assume the appellations or badges of

Brahmans and attend at nuptial and other ceremonies. They do not adopt chelas or disciplines, but their office is hereditary and descends from the father to all the sons; they partake both of the food which is dressed and of the cup which flows freely. In Dungarpur an order of priesthood is said to have been recently started; the priest is styled *Bhagat*, abstains from flesh and wine, and declines to take food from the hand of a Bhil unless he too be a *Bhagat*: his house can be recognized by the flag which is fixed to it.

The minstrels of the tribe are called *kamarias* or *dholis* and assume the garb of the *Jogi ascetic.* They play on their rude instrument, the guitar, and, accompanied by their wives, attend on the occasion of births, when they sing Bhil hymns to Sitla Mata, the protectress of infants. Then *bhopa* or witch-finder has already been mentioned; he appears to belong to the tribe and his office is generally hereditary. Ordinarily, he is not much cared for, but when he becomes "possessed", the hills obey him and usually give him what he asks for.

Festivals

The Holi, Dushhra and Dewali, festivals are observed and excess. It is kept up for ten days or more; dances take places always, stop travellers till they release themselves by paying a fine. At all festivals the men dance a ring dance called *ghanna* or *gher*. The drumers stand or sit in the centre, and the dance revolve in a circle with sticks in their hands which they strike alternately against those in front and behind; time is kept with the drum all through, and as the performers get more excited, the pace increases they jump about widely, their long hair falls down, and then one of them disengages himself and indulges in a pas scul inside the circle.

Gavri is celebrated is a dance-drame form lasting for forty days during the rainy season. It is essentially a ritual activity with a strong sacred content. The story centres around Shankar and Parvati. According to mythological legend, once Bhasmasur went into mediatioṅ of lord Shankar. Shankar was so much pleased with his devotion that he gave him a *'Bhasmi-Kada'* a kind of bangle, which could burn any one to death. In a flash of joy, he tried to apply it on Shankar himself and make Parvati his consort. However, Vishnu in the guise of Mohini came to his rescue and eventually killed Bhasmasur. While Bhasmasur was dying, he begged Vishnu that in some way his name should be immortalised. In his magnanimity Vishnu blessed that *Gavri* dance shall be performed to perpetuate his memory.[26]

On behalf of the villagers, the village *Bhopa* (Priest) seeks permission from the goddess for holding the festival. Generally, a village gets permission once in three or four years. Once the goddess blesses the devotees through the *Bhopa* (by way of sending him into a trance) to go ahead with the celebration, the *Gavri* preparations commence. The invoking of the deity is a feature of the initial and the concluding ceremonies for the entire period.

The ritual commences on the day following Raksha Bandhan when sowing has been completed and the crops almost begin to sprout. It is an ideal season, with no work in the field, to worship various gods and goddesses which form the sacred pantheon of *Gavri*.[27]

The activities on a particular day start with the fixing of the Trishul (lance nor trident) in the central part of the village. The deity is seated at that spot with incantations and incense is offered by the Bhil *Bhopas,* Admits shouts of Jai Shankar Mahadev and Jai *Gavri* Mai the deities are assigned their place for the day. The participants gather around the place and the *Bhopa* gets possessed of the deity's spirit. Two assistance to the *Bhopa* invoke Amba Mata and Dharmadev and get possessed of their spirits. In the state of trance they keep on striking the iron chains over their shoulders. Their bodies snake and the state of their being transcends from the secular to the sacred. Their words come as pronouncements of the deities. The rest of the participants express their joy at the success of the *Bhopas* in invoking the deities and begin to dance around them with the *Bhopa* leading them, amidst the music of drum and mandal. After this initial ceremony, nearly 80 odd deities are also invoked. Some of these are local and regional.

The cultural life of the Bhils is also depicted through *Gavri,* The dance is performed in a circular form to the accompanyment of Mandal, *Thali* and *Dhol,* The folk dance drama is performed in the open air without any stage. The Budiya dancers anti-clockwise while other actors dance clockwise. The performance is so captivating that all persons irrespective of their age, sex and caste witness the show from morning till evening.[28]

In the post independence period, some dance directors have ventured to experiment with the form of *Gavri,* retaining its tribal actors, finer movements and rhythm for adaptations to the requirement of the modern theatre and to bring it to the national milieu of dance and drama. Whether this process of experimentation, between tradition and modernity, will bring into the national spectrum then pristine glory of tribal culture would be seen in times to come.

Each village has a team of amateur dancers and dramatists. All the acts are played by male actors. *Buriya* (Shankar) is the principal actor and leader of the show. *Rai* is the principal actress. It is believed that goddess Paravati herself witnesses the celebration. The actors abstain from drinks, sex and take only vegetarian food once in a day, for forty days the duration of *Gavri*.

An item is concluded when the actors in the item come before the deity, make a bow and receive the final blessing of the *Bhopa*. The Bhils begin the day's function at about 10 a.m. and conclude the day a little before the sun-set.[29]

These initial rituals mark the preparatory part for the more popular items to follow. The items presented are plays and skits based on mythological and historical events and community life. The actors playing the different roles may be classified into the following categories:

(1) Actors playing the role of deities and Gods. These are: Kalka, Shiva, Paravati, Ambav & Kantha.

(2) Actors playing the role of human beings like (*i*) Budiya, (*ii*) Rai, (*iii*) Kut-Kadiya, (*iv*) Kanjar Kanjri, (*v*) Mina, (*vi*) Nat, (*vii*) Khetudi, (*viii*) Shankariya, (*ix*) Kalbelia, (*x*) Paita, (*xi*) Baniya, (*xii*) Kalu Keer, (*xiii*) Jogi, (*xiv*) Garda, (*xv*) Kangujari, (*xvi*) Banjary, (*xvii*) Sikligar, (*viii*) *Bhopa,* (*xix*) Banwari, (*xx*) Goma, (xxxi) Baanjdi, (*xxii*) Phata Phati, (*xiii*) Bagli, (*xxiv*) Devar-Bhaujaai.

(3) Actors playing the Role of Demons: these are (*i*) Bhanwara, (*ii*) Khadaliya Bhoot, (iii) Hathiya and (*iv*) Bhinyavad.

(4) Actors playing the role of animals: These include (*i*) Suar (pig), (*ii*) Rinchdi (Bear), (*iii*) Nahar (Tiger) and (*iv*) Bandar (Monkey).

The final ceremony of the festival requires a clay elephant which is supplied by the local potters. The closing ceremony of *Gavri* is performed on First Navmi of Ashwini months. The clay elephant on which Mata Paravati is seated is given the fare well (Balawan) by immersing it into the water.

The *Gavri* party goes around performing from village to village, which are related through affinal ties and connected through business and ritual exchanges. The festival is a testimony of social solidarity that exists between the Bhils and other people inhabiting these villages.[30]

Settlement of Disputes

All disputes and quarrels are settled by *panchayats,* whose orders are absolute; the invariable punishment is fine. A man found guilty of treachery is indiscriminately plundered and ejected from the pal, but can re-establish himself by paying the fine awarded by the *panchayat* in his case.

The fine for murder is usually about Rs. 200 (local currency), and until it is paid, a blood feud is carried on between the relatives of the victim and the murderer. Fights between one community or aillage and another are also indulged in to avenge an affront or to assert some right. Before active measures are taken, the patriarch of the village is consulted and if he decide for war, the Kilki or Bhil assembly a peculiar shrill cry mad by patting the mouth with the hand is sounded, or a drum is beaten, which gathers together all the inhabitants of the pal, male and female, in an incredibly short space of time. Drinking is first indulged in and, when sufficiently excited, they sally forth with the women in front and, on arrival at the opponents village, an enouter is soon brought about by means of a shower of stones and abusive language. When, however, the parties are actually opposed the women draw on side, and the fight commences with bows and arrows; the women give the wounded drink and assistance. After the battle the usual *panchayat* assembles, and the feud is generally closed by the payment of a fine, in which case the opposing parties make friends by drinking opium out of each other's hand.[31]

Disputes between the Bhils of one State and those of another in Rajputana or between Bhils of Rajputana and those of adjoining portions of Bombay or Central India are decided by Border Courts—a form of tribunal described at page 67 *supra*. Sir alfred Lyall in his *Asiatic Studies* gives an amusing account of a portion of the proceedings of an imaginary Border Court which is examing the headman of a village regarding a recent foray—"A very black little man, with a wisp of cloth around his long ragged hair, stands forth, bow and quiver in hand, swears by the dog, and speaks out sturdily; 'Here is the herd we lifted; we render back all but three cows, of which two we roasted and ate on the spot after harrying the village, and the third we sold for a keg of liquor to wash down the flesh. As for the Brahman we shot in the scuffle, we will pay the proper blood-money. A slight shudder runs through the high-caste Hindu officials who record this can did statement; a sympathetic grin flits across the face of a huge Afghan, who has come wandering down for service or gang robbery into these jungles, where he is to the Bhils a shark among small pike; etc."

Customs Connected with Births

A peculiar beat of the *dhol* or drum (of which there is generally one in every village) announces a birth or when this is not done, the *guru* or some other person carries the news to relations and neighbours who assemble at the hut of the parents and present gifs according to their means or wishes. Among some clans the *Kamaria* or minstrel attends; he first places a small figure of a horse at the threshold of the door, and then, taking up his position just outside, sings a hymn to *Sitla Mata,* the goddess of smallpox, who is much dreaded by all the wild tribes. Occasionally an arrow is placed near the babe's bed to wad off the evil influence of *devils.* On the fifth day a ceremony for propitiating the sun takes place and is attended by relations. Flour is scattered in the yard of the house, and the mother, dressed out in holiday satire, sits facings the east with an arrow in her hand; sheer invokes the blessing of the sun of her child, and after the distribution of rabri (porridge) and liquor, the gathering disperses. The head of a male child is shaved when he is two or three months old, and the ceremony of naming takes place either as soon after birth as possible or when the baby begins to try and turn of its own accord. Brahmans are sometimes called in, but the mass of the Bhils never think of his services, and the ceremony is usually performed by the paternal aunt or maternal uncle of the child. The name may be taken from the day of the week, on which the infant was born e.g. *Dita* or *Ditya* (Sunday), *Homla* or *Homa* (Monday), *Mangala* or *Mangali* (Tuesday) and soon; or from the season of the year e.g. Vesat (the rains), or from some shrub e.g. Thaura or Thauri, the beautiful red flowering shrub common in the Hilly Tracts. A child bom in times of gladness may be called Moti (pearl) or Rupa (silver) or, as a term of affection, *Kaura* or *Kauri* (darling).[3] The distinctively Bhil custom of branding male children on the wrist and forearm (without which mark on arrival at Bhagwan's house after death, the Bhil will be punished nor refused admittance) takes place at any time from birth till twelve years of age; some of the Bhils in Dungarpur say that it makes the boy a good long-distance runner. On the first Holi festival after the birth, the maternal uncle brings a goat and some wine and clothes for the infant, the goat is killed and cooked, a morsel of meat and a sip of wine are given to the child, and the relations present share the rest of the repast. The parents also give feat at this Holi and present clothes to their female relatives.

The Law of Marriage

The tribe, though not absolutely so, is considered as one endogamous group, but those who live in the hills do not usually intermarry with those who reside in the plains, though this is not actually prohibited. On the other hand, the law of exogamy is strictly observed, i.e. a man must not marry within his own clan or got, or within two degrees of his maternal and paternal relations; nor is marriage permitted among persons believing in the same goddess, known as the *gotra devi,* but as a rule each clan or group has its own goddess.[34]

Polygamy

The marriage of two or more sisters with the same person is permissible, as is polygamy generally; indeed, the latter is not uncommon and is nearly always resorted to if the wife be barren, too ill to attend to housekeeping, or immoral.[35]

Divorce

Divorces are allowed but are rare. A man wishing to divorce his wife must, in the presence of some of his tribesmen, tear her sari or head-covering breadthwise, loudly proclaiming his intentions, he must bind in the cloth so torn at least one rupees, and the garment is then returned to the woman who carries it about as the charter of her new liberties. If, however, the cloth be torn lengthwise, or the woman leave without a formal divorce, as described above, and take up with another man, the latter has to pay a fine to her husband. In some parts the custom is for the man to tear a piece off his own turban and it to his wife, instead of tearing the latter's *sari*. The woman apparently cannot dissolve the bound of marriage in this same facile fashion, but it is reported from Jodhpur that she can leave her husband if the latter fail to maintain her; or is impotent, or is excommunicated or abjures Hinduism. Polyandry is prohibited.

Elopement

Elopement is most probably resented and retaliated, and the quarrel may be prolonged, but sooner or later a panchayat will be appointed to settle the dispute and will award compensation (never exceeding Rs. 100) to the girls's father. A hole is dug in the ground and filled with water; the girl's father and the man she eloped with each drop a stone into it, and the incident is closed. Should, however, an unearthed girl refuse to elope when asked to do so, the man will generally shout out in the village that he has taken so and so's daughter's hand, and woe betide him who dares to many her. On such occasions a panchayat assembles, and the girl is generally handed over on payment of double the sum that would have been awarded had she originally consented to elope.[37]

Betrothal Customs

Betrothal, as a rule, takes place before the girl arrives at a marriageable age, but it is not at all unusual for girls of mature age to be spoused, and in such cases marriage follows as soon as practicable. The father of the girl can himself take no steps for his daughter's marriage; were he to do so, suspicion would be aroused that there was something wrong with her. The proposal or the girl's hand must come from the suitor, or his father, and the dapa or price of the girl is settled between the parties; the amount is said to vary between Rs. 30 and Rs. 50. In Jodhpur, however, the *dapa* is the sum paid to the *Darbar* or the *jagirdar* or the *panch* or tribal council (as the case may be) for permission to celebrate the marriage. Everything having been arranged, the *sagai* or betrothal ceremony follows, or rather used to follow for it is not always observed nowadays. The custom in Mewar was to place the girl on the stool under which six piece were thrown, a rupee, a piece and a little rice were put in her hand and she threw them over her shoulder. In Banswara the boy's father made a cup of the leaves of the dhak tree and, placing it on the top of an earthen pot of liquor, put inside it two annas in copper coij; the girl's brother or some other boy among her relations, took the money and turned the cup upside down. The betrothal was then complete and it only remained for the assembled company to drink the liquor. The *dapa* or price money is usually paid between the betrothal and the date fixed for the marriage, half in cash and half in kind. If this is not done, the betrothal can be cancelled, as also when the prospective bridge groom contracts some incurable malady, but in the latter event the first refusal of the girl must be given to his younger brother, if any; and the same is the case if the young man die after betrothal but before marriage. If a boy wish to break off his engagement to a girl, he and one of his relations pluck a leaf or two off a *pipal* tree and throw them into then water with a stone; this custom is, however, more or less obsolete, and on such occasions a scribe is now usually called in and a written agreement drawn up.[38]

Marriage

The price money having been paid, ceremonies and rejoicings begin several days ahead of the date fixed for the wedding. A doll of clay, called *dardi,* pierced all round with needles is placed in the house of the bridegroom, but with what object is not clear; it is perhaps intended to represent the Bhil as the typical archer armed cap-a-pie with arrows. In some places a priest takes pit (a mixture of turmeric, flour etc.) from the bride's to the bridegroom's father, and the latter supplies the young couple with new clothes; the two families exchange gifts of flowers and jagri (a coarse brown sugar), and there is much feasting, dancing and singing in both villages on the day of the wedding, the bridegroom, having been well anointed with piyt and wearing the peacock's feather in his turban, sets out for the bride's house accompanied by all his friends.[39] At the borders of the village he is met by the bride's father who performs the ceremony of *tilak,* that is to say, marks the bridegroom's forehead with saffron, and makes the customary present of a rupee. On reaching the bride's house, the bridegroom has to strike the *toran* or arch erected for the purpose, with his sword or stick, and the *arti* or auspicious lights are waved up and down before him by way of welcome. The actual marriage ceremony, at which sometimes a Brahman and sometimes an elderly member of the bride's family officiates, consists in the young couple, the *skirts* of whose garments are tied together, sitting for some time with their faces turned to the east before a fire *(hom)* or a lamp fed with *ghi* (clarified butter), and then joining their right hands and walking round the fire four times. On the first three of these circuits (pheras) the bride takes precedence, while in the last the bridegroom leads. Subsequently the bride is often placed on the shoulder of each of heer male relatives in turn and danced about till exhausted. In the evening there is a great feast, *the fare* consisting of bread and goat's or buffalo's flesh. Wine is freely used; in fact, the belief is that without it there cannot be a perfect ceremony, and its reckless use has many a time caused riots, and instead of merrymaking there has been fighting. The married couple are provided with a separate hut for the night, while their friends get drunk. On the following morning the bride's father gives his daughter a bullock or a cow or any worldly goods with which he may wish to endow her and, after presenting the bridegroom's father with a turban, gives him leave to depart. Sometimes the bridegroom stays for three or four days and wears the *kangna* (a bunch of threads with a piece of turmeric fixed therein) on his right wrist.[40]

Widow Remarriage

Widow remarriage is common among the Bhils, the ceremony being called *natra* or *karewa.* After the funeral of a married man, his widow, if young, is asked by his relatives if she wishes to remain in her late husband's house or be married again, and if, as is usually the case, she wishes to be married again, she replies that she will return to her father's house. Should the deceased have left a younger brother, he will probably step forward and assert that he will not allow her to go to any other man's house, and then, going up to her, will throw a cloth over her and claim her; he is, however, not bound to take on his brother's widow, but it is such a point of honour that even a boy will usually claim the right. Similarly, the lady is not bound to marry her late husband's younger brother, but as a matter of fact she is almost always agreeable, if, however, she decline the match and subsequently marry some one else, the younger brother will probably burn down the latter's house and generally make himself objectionable until the usual *panchayat* intervenes and awards him some small sum as compensation for his disappointment.

If the deceased have left no younger brother, his widow returns to her father's house as soon as the period of morning is over, and stays there till she can find another husband. No formal ceremony is requisite, for a *natra;* the man takes a few clothes and trinkets to the widow, usually on a Saturday night, they join hands, and their relations and clansmen eat and drink together.

Customs at Death

When a death occurs, a monotonous beating of the *dhol* or village drum or if a smaller instrument, made of mud with the ends covered with goatskin and called *nandla,* summeons the neighbours, each of whom brings some grain in his hand. The *kamaria* or *Jogi* takes his post at the door of the deceased's house, the image of a horse and an earthen jar of water being placed beside him, and each visitor gives him the grain he has brought and, taking some of the water in his hand, sprinkles it over the image while invoking the name of the deceased.

The Bhils almost invariably burn their dead-body generally face downwards but infants are always buried. It is also the custom to bury the first victim to an epidemic of smallpox in order to propitiate *Mata* and if, within a certain time, no one else dies of the disease, the body is disinterred and burnt. It is reported from Jodhpur that those who have become *Kabirpanthi Sandhus* are always buried in graves six feet deep.

The corpse is covered with white cloth, and a supply of food in the shape of flour, *ghi* and sugar is placed by its side for use on the journey to the next world. The cremation generally takes place near some river or stream, and a small copper coin is thrown on the ground as a sort of fee for the use of the place. The ashes are thrown into the river two or three days later, and a cairn is erected on the spot where the body was burnt, a pot of rice being also placed there; if, however, there is no river in the vicinity, the ashes are merely heaped together and the pot of rice is placed on the top. The bones recovered from the ashes are thrown into some sacred stream, such as the Mahi where it flows by the temple of Baneshwar in Dungarpur, for until this is done the spirit of the deceased in supposed to remain on earth and aunt the surviving relations.[4]

The Bhils erect stone tables in memory of their male dead and, as a rule, the figure of the deceased is carried on the stone. He is often represented on horse back with lance, sword or shield, and sometimes on foot, but invariably wearing the best of long clothes, a style of dress he was quite unaccustomed in the flesh. This appears to be a relic of an old custom according to which the figure of a Bhil who met his death at the hands of a horseman was shown as on horseback, while that of a man who was killed by a sepoy carrying a sword and shield would be in long clothes and with these seasons in his hands. Tablets erected to boys bear a representation of a larger hooded snake and not a human figure.

The *kata* or funeral feast is given by the deceased's heir about ten or twelve days after the cremation, the fare consisting of maize, rice, the usual liquor, and sometimes the flesh of buffalo or goat; in Jodhpur, however, meat and liquor are said to be strictly forbidden and, in the case of a child, the feat is held on the third day. While the repeat is being prepared the near relations of the deceased shave one another. On the morning of this day the ceremony of the arid begins and lasts a considerable time. The *bhopa* or witch-finder takes his seat on a wooden platform and places near him a big earthen pot with a brass dish over its mouth; a couple of Bhils beat the dish with drumsticks and sing funeral dirges, and the spirit of the deceased is supposed to enter the heart of the *bhopa* and through him to demand whatever it may want. Should the man have died a natural death, the spirit will call for milk, *ghee,* etc. and will repeat the words spoken just before death, whatever is demanded is at once supplied to the *bhopa* who smells the article given and puts it down by his side. If the death was violent one, a gun or a bow and arrows will be called for, and the *bhopa* works himself up into a great state of excitement, going through the motions of firing, shouting the way-cry and the like. Subsequently the spirits of the deceased ancestors are supposed to appear, and the same ceremonies are gone through with them.[44]

In the evening it is the *Jogi's* turn; he receives a few seers of flour, on the top of which he places a brass image of a horse with an arrow and a small copper coin in front. Having tied a piece of string round the horse's neck, he calls out the names of the deceased's ancestors and significance to the heir that now is the time for him to give alms to their memory; the appeal is generally responded to, and a cow is given to the *Jogi* who is directed to-provide the deceased with food. The *Jogi* then cooks some rice and milk and pours it into a hole in the ground and, having added a powerful of liquor and a copper coin, fills up the hole again, other mystic rites follow and the ceremonies and with the usual hard drinking. On the following day the relatives of the deceased give a feast to the village, each member contributing something; the honour of providing a buffalo belongs to the deceased's son-in-law or, failing him, the brother-in-law or brother.[45]

Inheritance

A Bhil when dying can call his family about him and tell them how he wishes to dispose of his property; if he fail to do this, his wife and eldest son, provided they are on good terms, are joint heirs and support the other dependent members of the family, but if they are not on good terms, the widow inherits everything on the same conditions. In default of a wife or sons, a brother succeeds and so on in the male line; the daughters and other female relatives inherit only such property as is specially willed to them.[46]

GARASIAS

The origin of the Garasias has been a matter of conjecture by historians on Rajasthan history. The problem has become complicated on account of some historians confusing Garasia tribals with Grasya Chieftains Col. Tod came in contact with some Grasya chieflatin of Mewar and wrote that a Grasya chieftain was one who held land (gras) by grant (Patta) of the prince for which he performed service with specified quotas at home and abroad, unavailable at every lapse.[47] Thus a Garasia jagirdar had perspective right on land. He considered 'Garasia' to be derived from 'Gras' meaning subsistence.

The word 'Garasia' originated around the thirteenth century. There is no earlier mention of the word in literature or inscriptions. The literal and etymological meaning of the word 'Girsia' can be understood if we remember that it is derived from Girahia meaning a foresh dwelling people. The Persian word Groh[48] has led to the derivative Girahia which has become Garasia. It only suggests the Garasias has a 'tribal' character and inhibited the area where they are found. Their tribal character goes against their having originated by a mixture of different castes, as Erskine postulated.

Contribution of Garasias to Rulers of Mewar

Maharana Udai Singh, while making arrangements for war against Akbar, convened a meeting of tribal patels of *Bhomat* and devised a plan for defense. The *guerilla* tactics to leave the plain and take shelter in the hilly and forested areas were then adopted. The Garasia *Barwas* have recorded land grants to the tribals by the Maharana in lieu of the services rendered by the Garasias in resisting the inadrig army. The deeds of Mungla and Kaine, Garasia leaders of *Bhomat* and *Bhakar* respectively, in killing famous Mugal elephants Kadiro and Sabdaliya by posion around are preserved in Garasia tradition.

During the time of Maharana Pratap, there were two claimants to the Sirohi Kingdom Jagmal Sisodia and Rao Surtan, the former was supported by the Mughals and the later by the Rajputs and Garasia tribal chiefs of Girwar, Bhirtore and Bhakar (Looma, Vagta, Natha). Rao Surtan decided to attack Jaghmal at Datani. The battle of Datani, as famous in the history of Sirohi as Haldi Ghati, Khanwa and Panipat are in Indian history, witnessed the defeat of Mughal forces on Kartik II, V.S. 1640 (1583 A.D.). In this battle Sisodia Jagmal, Raj Singh, Koli Singh including 35 Rajputs from rao Surtan's Samra, Deora including 20 Garasias were killed.[51]

Maratha Period

The Garasia tribals as well as the local rulers of Mewar and Sirohi, the petty *jagirdars, thakurs* and nobles were regularly attacked and harassed by the Maratha army during 1755-1758 A.D.

When a levy was imposed on the tribals by the Mewar Maharana for payment of tribute to the Marathaas, the patels of Jamudi and Bekaria in *Bhakar* and *Bhomat* called the tribal *panchayat* and decided not to pay the levy but to help the *jagirdars* and *thakurs* against the Marathas.[52]

1857 Revolt and Garasia Tribe

The dissatified jagirdars joined by the tribals became at part of freedom struggle. At Erinpura the nobles caught hold of Lt. Conoly, in command of the cantonment. Maharao Shiv Singh ordered Niamat AH Khan to proceed to Erinpura to help Lt. Conoly. Niamat Ali Khan finding it difficult to fight with the mutineers, promised to promote them, also heavily bribed Abbas Ali and Illahi Buv who were with the tribals.[53]

Economic Structure

Valro (shifting Cultivation)[54]

The hilly and forest regions left about 15 per cent of the total land in *Bhakar* as cultivable for agriculture. The Garasias came to attach great value to cultivable land and started reclaiming agricultural land by clearing forests once a year in the winter season. They practised controlled forest burning so that grass and minor forest produce were not destroyed recklessly and developed it as part of their ritual offering to *Magra Vavsi* (Maountain God). The Garasias believed that by offering fire bath to the *Magra Vavsi,* they would appeare the forest god who would reward them by producing bumper crops. It was also their belief that *valro* made the land soft, increased fertility of the soil helping proper germination of seeds, elimination of weeds and *Udai* (Pests). The burnt ash acted as manure. They firmly believed that burning of forest not only retained moisture in the soil but also facilitated quicker growth of the crop as also of the forest.

The Garasias developed agricultural practices which utilised soil of the gorges and slopes of hills by embanking successive terraces. The making of embankments and terraces has been interwoven with their belief system. They think that this practice is likely to please their *Khetar Vavsi* (field god) who would store enough water for them in the fields and bury the demons of drought, under the embankments. Today we can justify it on rational grounds, as suitable to the topography of *Bhakar*, hilly area. The successive terraces helped in the proper retention of rain water and reduce soil erosion.

Religious Rites

The Garasias depended on agriculture as their mainsty. Their entire energies were directed towards getting the maximum yield from land. Agriculture crops were likely to be destroyed by climatic vagaries, insects and pests, floods etc. The tribe naturally attributed these misfortunes to the displeasure of gods of climate, field and land. They developed practices to appeare the various gods connected with agriculture by offering sacrifices.[56]

At the time of garavana, 20 kg. of Churma is prepared and all Garasias assemble to participate in the ceremony. At the time of gajara green earheads of grains are baked in fire called *kol* and offered to *vavsi*. At this occasion they also worship *kala* and gora *bhairon*. Similarly, at the time of *mand* the Garasias would not forget to worship *nag* and other *vavsies* (local deities), Matar, Churma and lapsi (all cooked food preparation) from new grain are offered to *aag* (fire), *pewar* (air), *gune; nag* (corn god) after harvesting of eacy crop, the most significant offering of first fruits[57] (grain or vegetable) is brought to the bhomia, bhakar and other vavsies. No Garasia, not even the Government officials shall use any produce without offering the first fruit and grains to other god.

The religious rites, omens and tabooes followed during agricultural operations reflect the importance attached by the Garasias to various gods and goddesses.

Tabooes

The Garasias have lived for ages under blind beliefs and superstitions. Some of the restrictions and tabooes practised by them at the time of various agricultural operations are worth recording.

Women during their menstruation period are prohibited entry into the agricultural field at the time of sowing and threshing operations. They believe violation of this taboo gives not only rise to various crop disease like *kabiro, geru* or *kalio* but also lowers yield. The sacredness of the *lata* is enforced by refusing entry to men or women with shoes on or without hear or aged turbon or any other cloth covering head.[58]

For the same reason a number of other restrictions were also enforced on entry of men and women if they had become pollued. A cotton thread is used to cordon off the *lata* with four iron nails, one in each corner.

Omens

The Garasias observe haikan or heman (omens) in agricultural operation. At the occasion of horkadavi, garvana and jarvana or pan and irrigating the fields, the entry of an *andha* sakka (a kind of raptile similar to a snake having two mouths) in the field in considered as auspicious and similarly a chance breakage of jihroo at the time of ploughing juhroo is believed to forecast a bumper harvest.[59]

When a cultivator goes for sowing the field the chirping of sibri on his left, *kanho* or *bhero* (a kind of bird) on right side in a good omen, on the other hand coming across black "snakes, empty water pots, sterile women and widows, gripping of *duski* (a kind of bird) in front or on right in considered a bad omen for all occasions. At the time of bavni if a cultivator comes across a man carrying a head-load of fire wood it is considered in auspicious; if a bullock delivers pokula (dung), it is considered a good omen whereas if the bullocks urimates it is a bad sign. If a Garasia faces same bad omen before starting any agricultural operation he returns, rests for a while, remembers his almighty god and then proceeds to conduct the agricultural operations. These various beliefs and rituals have brought homogeneity not only at the micro level but also at the macro regional basis among the Garasias.[60] The religious practices, omens, taboos and beliefs have permitted into their society so deep that they have become the strong traditions in their economic life.

Farm Technology

Living in distinct and secluded hilly areas the Garasias are still accustomed to traditional farm technology. For ploughing purposes the wooden ploughs along with primitive tools are still in use. For irrigation purposes the system of pawati, saran, cha-ras etc. are in vogue. Only a few of the Garasias would think of installing rahat (persion wheel) for irrigation purposes. The use of modern farm technology has yet to find its place among the Garasias. The acceptance of chemical fertilizers, high yielding seed varieties, pesticides and insecticides have not yet gone into their general practice.

Most of the Garasias grow coarse grains like maize, *jawar*, barley, *kuri* (Panioum milaccum) *Kodra* (Paspalum scrobicultum) and malicha (Eleusine Coracana). Some types of crops like *Kulath, betri, Karra,* sample, *mal, sal,* etc. are also being produced by the Garasias. In recent years the Garasias have started cultivating wheat, rice, gram lentil, peas, mung and urd etc.

Animal Husbandry

In the absence of mechanical, electrical power, animal power, remains the backbone of Garasias agriculture. The animals are reared to provide power, transportation, manures and fuel. The tribe has developed various bonds with animals. A pair of bullocks, cows, sheep and goats are the main varieties of livestock kept by the Garasias. The types of animals, methods of rearing them customs and religious ceremonies, festival, sacrifices have almost the same pattern in all the Garasia pattas (region). Cows, goats and bullocks remain a medium of exchange in important social functions and marriage ceremonies. The bullocks are the main draft animals being harressed to carts, plough and employed for other purposes. Cow, buffaloes, sheep and goats supply milk, meat, wood and skin and goats are used for sacrifices to the gods, *vavsies* and *veers*.

The live stock has been one of the most valuable assets for the Garasias tribe; every house owner takes special care of them. Considerable vigilance is kept while driving cattle to and from forests. The *pesw vavsi* in worshipped by the Garasias since he is believed to avert danger to the animals ensuring safety and protection from wild animals.

Dhamino (Fishing)

The Garasias catch fish from the *nadi* (pond), *valoo* (rivers and tank. For this they adopt various methods. These area: johoomario (with the help of a piece of cloth), (a) Omemario (shooting by arrow) and (c) chhal (by forming small puddles in river bed and mixing dry powder of hingoni, kusum and cactus or thokar branches with water so that fish become blind and come to the surface.

Maid (Honey)

There are expert bee-keepers in the tribe, who have specialised in the art of not only collecting honey but also of controlling bee-behaviour. They use honey not only in diet but also for treating various diseases.

Social Structure

Clan System

The Garasias are organised into clans. Each clan traces its decadence to a legendary common founding ancestor who lived in the distant past. The clan nature of the Garasia depends on the individual substance as colour of body, eating habits and other biological regulations. A clan is further sub-divided into sub-clans called *adakh* (gotra). All persons belonging to a clan and its various *adakhs* regard themselves related to a common source and therefore form an exogamous group. The *adakh* names of a clan are its own monopoly and no two clans can have common *adakhs*. Marriage relations are possible only among different clans. The *adakh* of the Garasias may be named after plants, trees, vegetables, animals, memorable incidents, etc.[61]

The Garasias of different clans live, for the most part, in separate phalies of a village. Every Garasia must indicate his *adak* as part of his name thereby maintaining his social identity. A person is related to all those who bear the same adakh name. This practice enables them to enforce the exogarnous injections at the time of marital contacts. Thus the clan among the Garasias becomes primarily a social class. The women of a clan and its sub-clans are considered as sisters.

The clan goddesses are envoked at the time of all ceremonial occasions. Each clan has its own clan goddess.

Inheritance

Property after the death of a father is equally divided among his sons by the village elder or panchas and in case of dispute, by the tribal panchayat. The Garasias youth generally prefers to live separately after marriage and he is given a little portion of land by his father. The youngest son, even after marriage, has to stay with his parents. He gets some extra share in land and cattle wealth on account of being youngest, he gets the house of his father which is not divided. A grand son is not entitled to share, but he receives equal share if his father has died earlier. The daughters are not entitled to inherit their father's property, but they can share the animal wealth. Even in case of service marriage, the son-in-law, in the event of father-in-law's death, is not entitled to inherit property. Even if a man were to transfer land to his daughter through a registered deed in his life time this transfer shall have not legal value in the eyes of tribal law.

The Marriage System

Marriage among the Garasias is considered essential for both boys and girls. A Garasia must marry as marriage enhances his status. He will not hesitate to run into debt to get a wife. Marriage and children are considered essential for happy and prosperous life. Among the Garasias the age of a man is calculated by his physical appearance, strength and capacity to earn.

The marriage rules are guided by the tribal norms which forbid marriage outside the tribe and permit it outside the *adak* and do not allow it within the same village. In case of marriage outside the tribe, the guilty man is ex-communicated and put in *nanki jyat*.

Marriage among the Garasias lays special emphasis on consent of both the parties. Whether a marriage is an arranged one by elopment, consent of both the parties is essential. Normally the Garasias value matrimonial relations which are fairly firm in the eyes of tribal law and morality.[62]

No child marriage or infant betrothal in prevalent now amongst the Garasias though it might have existed in olden days because frequent reference are seen in folk song.

Young boys work hard so that they could pay dapa to get a wife. The girls father is paid because he losses an earning member or assets of his family. Secondly, the female sex ratio is lower among the Garasias and in further imbalanced because of polygamy. The demand for girls is much more than the availability hence the girl's price is paid in the form of *dapa*. *Dapa* is exempted only in cases where a man asks his son-in-law to stay with him on account of the absence of male-heirs. Such a marriage is called service marriage.

Monogamy and Polygamy

Monogamy is largely prevalent among the Garasias. The economic status of such Garasias is better than others. They have a house sufficient to accommodate a second wife and they are often village headmen *'patel'* who consider it a symbol of prestige to keep two or more wives.

Sometimes second or third marriage become justifiable when the earlier marriages do not result in the birth of a son.

Types of Marriages[63]

Morbandiya: In this system drums are played and it is also known viva, *lunga wala* or *Mandha wala* marriage. It is recognised as *mota* (important) marriage. Here the bride sits on 'path' for at least 5 or seven days and performs customary functions. Here a wooden structure known as *'manda'* is prepared with at least two hundred bamboos and nine *khulta* (wooden nails of salar tree) at the place of marriage ceremony. For an unmarried girl, nine pillars are used which symbolise-air, water, earth, sky and fire, *hamalaji, gotraj, dharamraj* and *patta.* To add importance to the marriage ceremony, a set of five earthen pots *benga* ascending order are placed with each pillar. These five vajja (pots) are given to sister, *bhuva*-mother's sister, aunt and helat (village haukidar) this is called benyo marriage.

Detwariya Marriage

It is performed on *ditwar* (Sunday) only. This is performed without dhol and the marriage expenses are about half or even less than the morbandhiya marriages.

Melbo Marriage

Keeping in view the poverty among the Garasias melbo marriages have been devised with a view to minimize the marriage expense. Under this system, barat (marriage party) does not go to the bride's house by the bride goes to the house of the bridegroom, without singing any wedding song.

This marriage is an indication of the strength of the bridegrooms party which compelled the bride's parents to surrender their daughter at the bridegroom's door.

Service Marriage

A man who does not have a son, wants a devoted boy who may manage his field and other affairs during his old age. He then wants to marry his youngest daughter to a boy who is willing to stay in his house. This is called service marriage. Here the father of the boy and the patel have to give a guarantee about the good behaviour of the boy and an assurance that he shall maintain the house as his own, shall cultivate the field, keep all the family members happy and shall pay regards and respect due to all the members.

Natra Marriage

Natra (Widow remarriage) among the Garasias is not considered bad. The widow to take initiative to search a suitable man who may marry her. Once the matter is decided she informs her father, who on fixed day, goes to the boy's house along with his daughter *Patels* of both the sides decide about *natra* marriage No specific ceremony is celebrated. *Natra* is also permissible for divorced ladies though it is a very complicated affair.

Ata-Sata (Marriage by Exchange)

Hami hatia (Ata Sata) is also another type of marriage prevalent among the Grasias. It is a marriage by exchange of their sisters by two young men. This type of marriage is done when both parties do not have money to pay for *dapa,* and have sisters to exchange. The consents of the girls are necessary.

Nahtta or Tarna (Elopment)

Elopment is the most common form of marriage among the Garasias and needs some what detailed description. This type of marriage is popular because of its romance, easy consent, quick decision for marriage and its being less expensive. Elopement may be with consent of both the parties (Nahtta) or may be with out consent (tama) Elopments are pre-planned and need long preparation. It has been accepted as the most convenient method of marriage because it is based on consent of both the parties and is more economical. Matrimonial relations have tended to be stable among the Garasias as the frequency of divorce is very little.[64]

Marriage Performances

Among the Garasias there are number of performances before actual marriage. The important ones are the following:

1. Hangai
2. Gurgi
3. Parla
4. Nutrave
5. Bethvna
6. Pitti
7. Vanola
8. Mande
9. Jan hidia
10. Gam-gadre
11. Bari-Kade

Birth and Childhood

Some women among the Garasias, on account of past traditions and empirical observations, are able to foretell the birth of boy and girl after observing the movements of the pregnant mother. It is firmly believed by the Garasias that generally the deliveries during *Shukla Paksha* (Bright nights) will lead to the birth of a boy when during *Krishna Paksha* (dark nights) will lead to the birth of a girl. They also believe that miscarriages, diseases, sterility of women, birth of girls etc. are due to the annoyance of some malevalent spirits or disfavour of some vavsies or due to the evil eyes of a witch.

Naming Ceremony

Naming Ceremony is always arranged at the holi festival when all the girls of the neighbouring houses are invited for selecting a good name for the newly bom baby.

Death

Women do not attend the funeral procession or cremation. They sit outside the home and bewali loudly. A pregnant lady will neither attend a morning ceremony nor will she be allowed to eat any thing prepared in *nyat*.[65]

To announce a var drum is beaten in a special way for three times and not more. On hearing var drum all the people of the village and neighbouring village leave their work and gather in the house of the dead. When all persons have assembled the dead body is kept on the *tikkti*. A coin is put in the mouth of the dead alongwith three *rottas* (baked bread) on the chest to be paid as tax in the cremation ground. Having completed all the formalities the wife is called for the last touching ceremony of the husband.

During the funeral processor one of the nearest male relatives will carry fire and mairje in earthen posts.

In case of a death by small pox and snake bite corpses are buried and not burnt. Burning of body is avoided to please *heetla mata* goddess of small pox so that more small pox may not visit the habitation.

The *bhopas, devata* and *dakan* are not burnt but burned in the ground. It is believed that *devata* and *dakan* after death turn to khatri and moghi respectively and they are sometimes worshipped, hence they should not be burrt.

Social Life

The Garasias enjoy *perab* (festivals) and *mello* (fair). Mainly there are three types of fairs:

(*a*) Gamero-mello-Fairs organised at the level of village where all the villagers participate. Such mellas are held in honour of Bharav, Patavsi and on the occassion of holi, diwali and navratra.

(*b*) Patta-ro-mello-Fairs organised at the level of a patta is honour of bhakar, magra and other territorial gods. There are held in different villages of a patta by rotation. The mella is announced by the beat of drums in a special manner a day before the schedule date of fair.

(*c*) Melkho-ro-mello-In this mella the Garasias assemble along their entire family, they carry with them cooked food of juggery, mairye or other things to prepare food in the mella itself. These mellas are specially colourful in the nights.[66]

Calendar Year of Perab (Festivals)[67]

The calender year of the Garasias starts from akha teej. The sequence festivals is:

1. Akha teej
2. HanghBalev
3. Navratra
4. Deshara
5. Dhanteras
6. Diwali
7. Kali Kartika
8. Paushukla dooj
9. Hita Choudas
10. Holi
11. Hacli hata
12. Gaur

1. ***Akha Teej:*** The *Navover* (New Year) begins with *akha teej* (on the third day of the bright half of the month of Baisakh). All accounts start from this day and old

dues are paid up and renewed, if necessary for the next year. Even all mortage deeds are written on this day. The day is considered auspicious and every one tries to make the whole year auspicious by some activity or by some indication observing heman.

2. ***Hang (Sangh):*** It is a festival of devotion and worship. *Hangh* is taken to arnya mahadev, mataji and Mt. Abu (Nakki). It is generally taken on *Purnima,* on that day a fast is observed in the honour of god. The earliest hang (Sangh) that went, could be traced from barwa's record of the 17th century called *Poonam-ka-hung.*[68]
3. ***Balev (Raksha Bandan):*** *Balev* literally means a new string. This festival to be connected with king Bali. On *balev* (Raksha bandan) the villagers go to the patel to greet him. Patel ties a rakhi to the villagers and offers juggery or *Churma* to them, over and above this practice, it is celebrated in the usual manner as among the Hindus. A sister offers two coconuts and ties a balev on the right hand of her brother. The brother accepts with respect and love. They prepare lapsi, *Churma* or *malpua.*
4. ***Norta (Navratra):*** The Celebration of this festival is held from the first to the ninth day in the bright half of Asoj. Fifteen days before the norta (navratra), the villagers assemble and decide whether they have to take *navratra* or not. It is organised at the village level by the people.

   This is nine days long festival. On the fist day they establish the *navratra* in the temple of the family goddess, it is called thap. Out of various *bhopas* in village, one *patvi bhopa* will be incharge of all activities for nine days. On the second day, the bhopa and villagers go to the house of *patel* where a *kolha* (Pumpkin) is cut as symbolic of the sacrifice of a buffalo in olden days.[69]

On the remaining days the Garasias visit the elders in the village. On the ninth day of the *navratras* the bolavu or boravnu ceremony is performed where a goat is sacrificed to please all the remaining gods.

5. ***Deshera:*** On the Deshera day a number of goats are sacrificed for goddessess Chamunda, Kali and other family goddesses.
6. ***Dhanteras:*** It is celebrated on the thirteenth day of dark fortnight at *Kartika.* Since morning the cows are given bath and in the evening *gughari* are prepared and taken. A lamp is also lit at night.
7. ***Diwali:*** Deepawali (diwali) is celebrated with full enjoyment. A special type of lamp out *tubla dubi* (gourd) is prepared. On the next day festival is celebrated. The cattle could enter anybody's field and no one will stop them from grarying or drive them away. They pray for the safety of their cattle wealth and request the goddess to protect the cattle from thieves and tigers.
8. ***Hita Chaudash:*** It is celebrated on the 14th day of the dark fortnight of Magh month. It is celebrated only by all cultivators and labourers. Each person brings his own flour, gour and ghee to prepare *churma* and all of them take a joint lunch after worshipping land, wells and also gods and goddesses connected with agriculture.
9. ***Holi:*** Holi is celebrated with great joy, exuberance of mirth and dancing. About 15 days before the Holi, the Holi *bhopa* decides the day of the commencement of dancing. Once the holi dance has begun it continues for the whole fortnight.

   On *Poornima* of *Phalgun* the girls go round the holi with *jaivare* with the baskets on their head, they dance and make seven rounds of *holi danda.*

10. ***Gaur:*** The villagers decide whether they would celebrate gaur festival or not, depending on the property of crop. It is observed from the 7th day of the dark half upto the full moon day in chaitra. Gaur festival is one of the most important festivals of the Garasias. It is unique in several ways. The gaur dances continue upto poonam. This festival provides an opportunity to all young boys and girls to make contacts with a view to finding their life partners.

Food Habits

The Garasias are non-vegetarians. Their staple food is maize, jawar, wheat and rice. Earlier they used to have plenty meat of wild and domesticated animals in the forest area, but with the passage of time and new restrictions on wild life hunting, meat has become a diet for special occasions. The most common food among the Garasias is *rab* or *doh.* It is prepared by mixing flour with butter milk. Broadly their food can be classified in the following categories:

(a) ***Navanikhoo:*** Special preparations on festive occasion are made. Dishes like churma, matar and sweet lapsi, malpua, etc. are prepared on festivals and also at the time of marriage, births and an arrival of guests.

(b) ***Khanva (Daily Preparation):*** There are three types of breads *roto* (bread of maize), *rota* (bread of wheat), *roti* or *pania* (bread of maize wrapped in the leaves of khakhara palas) tree and baked. It becomes very delicious if eaten with milk. They mix spices with flour in order to make the dishes more tasty.

(c) ***Kodio:*** Dried ubara (Fruits) of gular, peeplo, kharyor, and varla tree are mixed with maize or wheat flour and taken during days of calamities and famines.

(d) ***Food prepared:*** at the time of nyat (death ceremony) is called geh. It is mainly lapsi, khichra and *dalia.*

They will also take wild vegetables and fruits in ample amount.

Use of Intoxicants (NESSO)

Drinking is common among Garasias except among children below 8 years. On festivals occassions, marriage parties and fairs they prepare wine by mixing the bark of *goriya, mahua, reejhadva, mal kakani* and *babul.*

Khobroo (House)

The Garasias have generally a house on the slopes of the hills nearest to the field from where he could watch his field and crop. After marriage every Garasia constructs a new house and likes to stay separately with freedom.

The ground plan of the house is normally rectangular, but it is raised from the ground so that rain water does not enter the house. It provides some safety from snake and other crawling insects. The plinth as made of rocky flat stones which are easily split lengthwise and widhwise as per the required thickness. The door generally faces the east, being the direction of the sun. It is also believed that eastern wind (Purbia hawa) also gives prosperity. The *bhitur* (walls) are made of small stones, mud bricks and joined with mud mixed with cow dung. Flooring of the house is also *kucha.* Some time bomboo is also used for frame work for construction of the walls which are plastered with mud on both sides.

Mendol (roof) is made of timber thatched with grass, leaves, bamboo or wooden stripes. Tiles are placed horizontally. Tiles are handmade and baked in open fire. These are coarse and red in colour. Raw tiles are prepared by mud mixed with straw and husk. These are pressed with finger. *Mendol* (roof) is supported with a vertical wooden pole in the middle which is called *thambla* or *koota.* The sloping roof protects over the walls and provides a sort of *pethal* (varandah) where the family members squat during the day and sleep during the night. The old persons normally sleep in these

Pethal (varandahs). The room serves for living, cooking and also storing the house hold goods.[70]

The house of a patel may be painted with red clay and that of the rest with white. Its sirge is bigger. He has two houses for emergency needs.

DAMOR

The Damor is a small tribe. They migrated from Gujarat state and are largely located in the Simalwara Block of Dungarpur district of Rajasthan adjoining Gujarat. The Damors have a population of 43,612 (1991).[71]

The Damors of the border of Gujarat and Rajasthan in the district of Dungarpur speak Gujarati of mixed form. A majority of them speak *Vagri* which is local diilect spoken by rest of the population of Dungarpur district.

The Damor are taken to be a branch of the Bhils. The identification of Damors is largely due to habitation and forming interior villages on hills bordering Gujarat from where they migrated. Damor in the state of Rajasthan have been demarcated a separate identity. Damors also called Damarias and have no sub-groups.[52]

Clans (Moieties)

Damor have two moieties. One upper Damor and other lower Damor. Both groups treat themselves superior, but marital relations are restricted between them. Both the groups are exogamous and have their own clans.

Most of the clans have similarity with Rajput clans. They believe that their ancestors were Rajput and due to some social sin, they were debared from the caste and fallen into group of tribals.

Family

Damors prefer nuclear family in which father-mother and unmarried sons and daughters live together. Generally parents prefer to live with their youngest married son. Joint family is rare. They are matrilineal and partilocal.[73]

Life Style

Birth Rituals

In the Damors first delivery generally takes place in the house of girl's parents. The succeeding deliveries take place in the house of parents or at their own house. An elderly women of the family acts as midwife. Usually the period of confinement is limited to twelve days after the delivery. On the twelfth day the mother worships the sun with her relative and neighbours known as *"Huraj Puja"*. Sister of the husband has specific role to paly after the birth of the child.

Namkaran

The Damors invite Brahmin to perform the Namkaran ceremony. This ceremony is performed after the third or fourth month of the birth of the child.

The role of the *Bhuva* is important in the name giving. Damor usually name the child on the basis of week days or after ancestors.

Mundan

Like high caste Hindu *Mundan* ceremony is observed among the Damors. Generally the *Bhuva* accepts the hair of the new born. In this ceremony, *Bhuva,* presents cloths to the infant. Some presents are also given by relatives. When there is no male child in the family, a husband may either be permitted to marry another women or to adopt brother's or sister's son. Sometimes son-in-law can also be accepted as successor.[74]

Marriage Rituals

The marriage age varies between 12 to 15 years, both in case of male and female. The negative checks are clan exogamy, sapinda restriction i.e. there is no preference for cross cousin or parallel cousin marriage, they can not marry out of Damor tribe and a boy can marry a *Bhagat* or non-Gotra Damor irrespective of his category of orientation, *Dapa* or bride price has to be paid for marriage.

Polygamy does not exists in this tribal group, but exceptions can be seen. Pre-marital relations are not permitted in the society. In case of deviation of this rule, the offenders have been punished. The proposal for marriage is initiated by the parents of the boys. The instance of marriage by elopement can be seen. Generally marriage is performed by a Brahmin priest on Hindu pattern. Usually, after marriage the spouses live in a separate house.

Widow marriage is prevalent among Damors, generally levirate marriage is popular. If the husband younger brother refused to marry with his *Bhabhi,* then the widow can marry with other person of her choice. In widow marriage *Dapa* is also taken by bride father. The widow marriage is arranged in a simple manner.

Divorce is permitted in this tribal group, Husband and wife both can seek divorce. Husband wishing to seek divorce is allowed, but bound to compensate bride price to his wife. This *Jagda* is settled by the *Panch* of *Jati Panchyat*. If the divorce is sought by wife no compensation is paid. In such a matter no *Jagda* is taken for divorce.

Death Rituals

The dead body is cremated among Damors. The dead body of a child or that of a person died by smallpox is buried thirteen days of morning is observed. In the mourners house no food is cooked, food and drinks are supplied by near kin to the family. The first ten days after death is obseved as pollution period. On the 13th day the members of the tribe assemble at the residence of deceased person and turban tieing ceremony is observed and a feast also given to guests. The eldest son of the deceased also gets turbans called as *Sora-Pagdi* from the villagers, which is sign of his recognition for succession. In Damors ashes are dispersed in holy rivers or nearby ponds according to their economic status.

Occupation

The Damor economy is largely based on agricultural. Generally they have 3 to 4 bigha of land. The quality of land is poor. In hard times they go for labour. Out of working force 95.21 per cent were engaged in agriculture and rest of population in other occupations. Lack of education and poor agricultural techniques have kept the Damor economy largely to a stage of subsistence.

Religion

With the passage of time the Damor have accepted Hindu god and goddesses. Some of their deities are of local importance. These are *Kairing Mata, Kandia Mata, Dhuli Mata* and *Kalka Mata,* The Hindu gods worshipped are Mahadeo, Ganesh, Rama Krishna. Ganga and *Ranchodji*. They also worship Khatri Mata of Gujarat and sacrifices animal to her at the time of any epidemic among the cattle. This deity also assists in curing snake-bite.[78]

In many ways Damors have been Hinduised by the impact of *Bhagat* movement on their social life. The *bhagat* Damors do not eat any thing before bath. After bath, the offer prayers to their *Guru* and Hindu god, specially Ram and Krishna. They also observe fast on certain days. *Bhagat* Damors are strictly vegetarian and they do not take alcoholic drink.

Fairs and Festivals

Most of the fairs and festivals of Damors are the fairs and festivals of the High caste Hindus. The mode of celebration of festivals are similar of high caste Hindu. They do not have any special fair and festivals are their own.

Social Organisation (Traditional Panchayat)

In matter like out-casting a member, dispute over an extra marital relation, question pertaining to the formulations of reformation in the tribal organisations and feasts as part of social punishment are some of the main functions of the Tribal inter-village organisation consisting of 80 village.[79]

The Damor traditional panchayat can be seen at the level of clan and village. As the clan level, minor disputes pertaining to marriage and bridge price and brought. The head or chief of the *Panchayat* is known as *Mukhi* like the *Patel*. The village panchayat is usually convened to decide cases of development, land disputes, criminal cases, etc. The posts of *Mukhis* is hereditary. Now the cases are lodged in the law court, hence the power of traditional panchayats are decaying and their importance is decreasing.

Bhagat movement has effected their social life. They are fully vegetarian and do not take liquor.[80] The development programmes have effected their social life. With development programmes, their economic conditions has been improved to some extent. Effect of Urbanisation can also be seen on their social life. Their socio-economic life is changing.

KATHODIS

The Kathodis, also called the *Katkaris,* formerly a scheduled tribe of Maharashtra are now, a recognised tribe of Rajasthan also. In Rajasthan, the Kathodis have an insignificant number and have been culturally isolated from their own tribesmen and are trying to get assimilated with the other tribes of Rajasthan.

The heavy concentration is found in Kolaba, Thana and Khandesh districts of Maharashtra. The migrated members of this tribe in Rajasthan are mostly from Songarh and Nawapur villages of Khandesh districts in Maharashtra.

Both the names of the tribe; Kathodis meaning *Katha* or Catechu-makers and Katkari meaning a wood-cutter or a person engaged in occupations, like bamboo-cutting felling of trees, catechu-making and charcoal-making. The Kathodis have different stages of cultural development according to their different occupations.

Welling says that the Katkaris are people of the *Jungles,* who have no land of their own, no fixed, sedentary professions, they are hunters, coal makers, gatherers and sellers of forest produce, fresh water fisherman, field labourers and agriculturists.

The Kathodis are the people of the Hills and low Forest. They are habituated to lead an unsettled nomadic life. Nomadism has become a cultural trait with the Kathodis. They are fond of wandering and can leave their habitations on the slightest encouragement. They are so fanciful that on very poor promises they can migrate to any place. They are experts and are known for their frugality and endurance. The Kathodis are crazy after wine and a major portion of their earnings is spend on drinking. The tribe is known as one of the most economically backward tribes of India. Their conditions in Rajasthan are even worse than the Seharias who are the most under-developed of all the tribes in Rajasthan.

Early Migration in Rajasthan

The Kathodis were brought in Rajasthan by some Bohra Forest Contractors for employing them as forest labourers for making *Katha* from *Kher* trees. The Bohra contractors persuaded some 300 families of Kathodis to depart from their native place to seek fresh employment in the forests of Western Udaipur. In the initial stage only males visited the site of contract and worked in the Kher Forest. They returned to their native place when the Katha-Season was off. This process was inconvenient to the Kathodis and the contractors promised many other facilities. On his high promises many Kathodis migrated with their families. In the beginning they were employed in the forest areas of Badli and Mahadi villages of Kotra Bhomat in Udaipur district, where they worked with tooth and nail and received rations which were not enough to keep them up. For many years they lived in the vain hope that conditions would improve and lived in primitive conditions.

At present the Kathodis are reported to dwell in Shabad village of Kotah district and in some villages of Udaipur district. In Udaipur district they are reported to reside in Bodadar, Juda, Samija and Vas villages of Kotra tehsil and Manipur, Madra, Ambasa, Ambvavi and Daiya villages of Jhadol tehsil. But in the beginning they were brought in Badi and Mahdi villages and from there they got scattered over a number of villages.

The conditions of the Kathodis in the Kher forest became worst when the forest exhausted and these poor people were left at the end of their resources. This involved the Kathodis in a struggle for existence, the consequences of which are seen in the various aspects of their life even today. Their standard of living is extremely low and many of them still live to the subsistence level.[84] Their condition has further been worsened by the primitive conditions under which they earn their living. When they began to starve they decided to go back to their native place in Maharashtra.

Social Organisation

In Maharashtra the Kathodis are divided into two sub-sections, viz., *Dhor Kathodi* and *Sonkathodi.* The *Dhor Kathodis* is completely namadic section and leads an unsettled life. The following exogamous division can be seen in Maharashtra :- (1) *Vardi Jagoda,* (2) *Vaghira Nadagulyr,* (3) *Bhenda,* (4) *Pawar,* (5) *Dhuma,* (6) *Lakhan,* (7) *Niwar,* (8) *Misal.*

K.J. Save mentions in his book The Warlis' that the Ketkari form only the bottom of the social ladder of the original tribes. The Kathodis are considered to be inferior to some of the aboriginal tribes like *Warlis, Dhodias, Dublas, Konkans* and *Kolis* of Maharashtra. In the same way they are treated as inferiors by the Meena. Bhil and Garasia tribes in Rajasthan. These do not dine with the Kathodis, not accept water from them.

Family

Among the Kathodis the family is the unit of the Social organisation. Thus the individual is primarily responsible to his family. A Kathodi family is a self-centred family. It was observed that a male separates himself and forms another family after he gets married. It is common that the Kathodi groom, after marriage, joins the family of the father-in-law and lives with him and cultivates his lands.

A Kathodi family is simple, nuclear, patriarchal family in which the male dominates over the female. The head of family does not allow his wife to earn a living, but his unmarried daughters are allowed to do so. In Kathodis married female are not allowed to go for the collection of forest produce, but they help in other things relating to their earnings. For example they help their husbands by making bundles of bamboos cuts, and fetches it down from the top of hills where the bamboo is cut. She also cleans the forest produce. Likewise she works on the *Musli* at home but for earnings as such she never works. The wives are loyal to their husbands. No case was reported by any kathodi or other persons of the area relating to the elopement 6f the married or unmarried. Not a single Kathodi divorced or left his wife since their rehabilitation in the area. This shows that family bond is strong among the kathodis.

(i) ***Birth:*** Customs related to birth are same for male and female child. Six days pollution period is observed after the birth of a child. Mother and the child are confined to a hut for six days. Nobody is allowed to enter in that hut except mother in law and sister-in-law who look after the new born baby and mother. On the sixth day the mother is given a perificatory bath. A ceremony called is also observed on the twenty

days, on *surya puja* the mother and child took bath and worship the family deities.

(ii) Marriage: Among Kathodis marriage in the same Kul is not permitted. Divorce and widow marriage is allowed. The marriage of the son or daughter is decided by the parents. The father of the boy looks for a girl for his son. To settle the marriage the father of the son goes to the home of the girl and settled the date of the marriage. At the time of the betrothal the bride's father puts red-mark *Tilak* or *Tika,* on the forehead of the bridegroom. The *Dapa* or Bride Price ranging from Rs. 21 to 100 is paid to the bride's father by the bridegroom. The marriage is celebrated by community dancing. Some hindu rituals have been adopted by the Kathodis in their marriage ceremonies. A *Mandap* is erected with the support of four sticks of *Saldi* Tree and covered by leaves of *Jamun* Tree. Under this *Mandap* the marriage is completed, the burning fire being its witness.

Generally, marriage takes place within the next three or four months of the betrothal. Men, woman and children join the marriage procession and go to the bride's home. Just after marriage the bridegroom takes the bride to his house to receive the blessing of the parents and other elderly members of the family.[87]

The married male, then leaves the family of his parents and with his wife forms his own family.

(iii) Death: The Kathodi bury their dead body. After the death, the deceased is carried to the burial ground by the sons or nearest relatives. They put the soil over the dead body. The Kathodi observe six days pollution period after the death of a person. During that period the sons or nearest relatives lead a simple life. After six days the relatives & friends assembles in the deceased house for drinking the liquor.

Clan and Totemism

In Maharashtra Kathodis having the same clan deity but different clans generally do not intermarry. But sometimes persons with the same do intermarry. *Bhopli* or *Phople* means betel-nut; but the people of this clan chew betel-nut, while in Hindu, clan totemism is observed. *'Vagh'* means a tiger; but the Vagh kathodi cldn does not hesitate to kill tiger. Thus the study of clans among Kathodis made by many anthropologists reveal that some clans are totemistic; others are names of the terriories and few other refer to profession, while some are the names of Maratha families or other caste like *Ahir, Jagan* and *Kali.*

Language and Literacy

In Maharashtra Kathodis speak Marathi dialect but in Rajasthan they have developed a new dialect which is a combination of Vagdi and Marathi. They pronounce common Marathi words like *Doam* (Two) *Dakhwa* (Show) and *Sanga* (Tell) etc.

Most of the Kathodis are illiterate. According to 1991 censes 5.80 per cent Kathodis were literate (9.61% males & 1.95% females).

Housing Conditions

A Kathodi House gives a typical appearance. Their huts are made of wood, grass and leaves. The hut is a wooden frame covered by grass and leaves. The roof is slanting on both the sides. The hut is generally of a height of 4 to 5 feet, with a narrow low entrance bearing no door. There are no windows to the hut. The hut is rectangular in shape; the length of the wall is about two to three feet up to top and the rest two walls make a shape of a Pentagon. The entrance is placed in any one of the pentagonal walls and this makes the front-elevation of the house. There are no separate places for sleeping, storing or cooking in the hut. In front of the hut generally a platform is raised which is square and is used to keep the fodder for animals and other things. The square platform rests on four wooden walls about 5 feet high hung in the air and is covered with a grass-shed, is supported to keep high with the help of bamboo and raw wooden frame. Their miserable condition is reflected through their derelict huts.

Religion

The Kathodis prefers Hinduism. Their deities are *Amamata* and *Kalka Mata*. They have their family deities. They do not have any village or regional deity nor do perform any worship rointly. The sacred specialist is from their own community who performs birth, marriage and death sites.

Fairs and Festivals

The Kathodis observe the local festivals with full of joy. They celebrate the festivals Holi, Diwali, Rakshabandhan and Navratri, etc.

Their cultural heritages also very rich and having special as other tribal groups. They have their own folk songs. Both men and women participate in dancing and singing during special occasions viz marriage, festivals and festivities. They also take actively part in the local fairs, they do not have any special fair.

Economy

The main economic resource of the Kathodis is forest. They were brought to Rajasthan for the preparation of *Katha* from *Kher* tree.

At present, due to the absence of Kher tree and strict forest policy, they are unable to do their traditional calling. The different occupations do not increase their incomes nor bring any stability in the earning. This shows itself in their restless haunts to cope up with the base requirements for existence.

The Kathodi economy is based on forest labour and forest produce. Thus, their primary occupation is forest labor and gathering and selling of forest produce, agriculture and agricultural labour being the subsidiary occupation. In Kathodis the family is the unit of earning.

Jati Panchayat

The Kathodi *jati Panchayat* is concerned generally with the control and regulation of relations between different members of society and to maintain tribal traditions, administration and rules. It consists of five persons selected by mutual consensus of the villagers. The head of the Panchayat is called *Nayak.* The cases of adultery and disrespect to traditional norms are delts with firmly and the guilty are fined. The amount of fine is generally spent on drinking and feasting by the *Nayak* and other members.

REFERENCES

1. Robert, Deliege: The Bhil of western India, National, Delhi (1985), p. 73.
2. Singh, K.S. (Ed.): Tribal Situation in India, Indian Institute of advance studies, Shimla, Vedic Index (1972), Vol. II, p. 24.
3. Tod, James: Annals and Antiquities of Rajasthan Vol. I-II Reprint, (1960), p. 86.
4. *Ibid.*, p. 103.
5. *Ibid.*, p. 106.
6. Hendl, R.S. : An account of Mewar Bhils, an artide on the Journal of Asiatic, Society Bengal, (1875), p. 34.
7. *Ibid.*, p. 39.
8. Carstairs, Morris: "The Bhils of Kotra Bhomat" an article in Eastern Anthropologist, (1954) Vol. VIII, p. 34.
9. Naht, Y.V.S. : Bhils of Ratanmal M.S. University Journal, Baroda, (1960), p. 51.
10. Mehta, Prakash Chandra: Bhart-Ke-Advisai, Shiva Publishers Distributors, Udaipur, (1993), p. 29.

11. Jain, Nami Chand: Bhi; Bhasha, Sathiya Aur Sanskrit, Hira Bhaya Prakash Indore, M.P. (1964), p. 42.
12. Roy, S.C. : Bhils of Mewar, Calcutta, (1924).
13. Mehta, Prakash Chandra: Changing face of Bhils, Shiva Publishers & Distributors, (1998), p. 74.
14. *Ibid.*, p. 79.
15. *Ibid.*, p. 83.
16. Symcox, A.M. : The History of Khandeshli Bhil, (1960), p. 42.
17. *Ibid.*, p. 51.
18. *Ibid.*, p. 53.
19. *Ibid.*, p. 64.
20. *Ibid.*, p. 92.
21. *Ibid.*, p. 94.
22. Chaudhary, N.D. and Vyas N.N. : "Banner: the Border district". Tribe, Vol. VII, No. 2, (1970), p. 10.
23. Bhanawat, Mahendra: "Bhil Jivan, Samaj Aur Sarokar" Rangaan, Jan. to June, (1992), p. 48.
24. *Ibid.*
25. Das, Shyamal: "Veer vinod" The Royal Palace, Udaipur Vol. I, p. 34.
26. Chauhan, B.R. and Chelawat, D.S. : "Bhil Gavri", Tribe (1966), Vol. VIII, No. 1, p. 7.
27. *Ibid.*, p. 10.
28. Das, S.T.: "Lifestyle of Indian Tribal, Gain Publishing House, New Delhi, (1989), Vol. III, p. 272.
29. *Ibid.*, p. 281.
30. *Ibid.*, p. 283.
31. Bairathi, Shashi : "Tribal culture, Economy and Health", A study of Bhils of Rajasthan (An unpublished study by Department of History and Indian culture, University of Rajasthan, Jaipur) (1993), p. 22.
32. *Ibid.*, p. 28.
33. *Ibid.*, p. 31.
34. Kumar, Pramod: "Fulkicons and Rituals in tribal life", Abinav, publications (1984), p. 78.
35. Debarat, Mandal: "Life and Culture of the bhils of Mlwa". Changing face of Bhils, Shiva publishing distributors, (1998), p. 73.

36. *Ibid.*, p. 76.
37. *Ibid.*, p. 85.
38. *Ibid.*, p. 93.
39. Vyas, Narendra; "Bhil Nari", Tribe, (1979), Vol. XI, No. 2-4, p. 41.
40. *Ibid.*, p. 44.
41. Sahay, Sachidanand : "Indian Costume, Coiffure and Ornaments", Munshiram Manohar Lal Publishers Pvt. Ltd., New Delhi (1975), p. 108.
42. *Ibid.*, p. 119.
43. Gulati, R.K.: "A Profile of Social Change among the Bhils of West Khandesh", Tribe, June (1970), Vol. VII, No.1, p. 22.
44. *Ibid.*, p. 33.
45. *Ibid.*, p. 34.
46. *Ibid.*, p. 37.
47. Col. James Tod, Annals and Antiquties of Rajasthan Vol. I, p. 133.
48. They lived in groups and stil follow the principles of;Giroh' (group cohesion and unity) Bajrang Lal Lohia in his book Rajasthan-Ki-Jatiya on Page 152 also suggested the word 'Giroh'.
49. Lt. Col Erskine, Garyetteer of Sirohi State, p. 255.
50. *Ibid.*, p. 318.
51. Rana Rao, M.S. Verses, pp. 677-727.
52. *Ibid.*, p. 411.
53. It is said that they were given five thousand rupees each and 25 bighas of land as told by Girasia Barwa Ram Singh.
54. Rajasthan State archives, Bikaner, Sirohi, record, Basta No.3, file No. 160 of 1931, p. 24.
55. *Ibid.*, p. 26.
56. *Ibid.*, p. 32.
57. Agryanyasti is as old as the vedas (offering of first fruit) Grihya Sutra Vi, 29, 2 ff, p. 36.
58. *Ibid.*, p. 38.
59. *Ibid.*, p. 40.
60. *Ibid.*, p. 41.
61. *Ibid.*, p. 44.
62. Marwar Raj Ki Mordhumshumari, Vol. I, p. 132.

63. *Ibid.*, p. 134.
64. *Ibid.*, p. 135.
65. Mahendra, B.I.: 'History and culture of Girasia' Adi Prakashan, (1985), p. 105.
66. *Ibid.*, p. 128.
67. *Ibid.*, p. 129.
68. *Ibid.*, p. 130.
69. *Ibid.*, p. 135.
70. *Ibid.*, p. 137.
71. Census (1991).
72. Sharma, Sheela : "Aadivasi Kala Parivartit Swarololp" Tribe, 1988, Vol. XX No. 1-4, p. 44.
73. Mathur, V.B.: "Folkways in Rajasthan", Himalaya an Publication, 1986 p. 91.
74. Mehta, P.C.: "Tribal Development"., Shiva Publishers, 1999, p. 30
75. Kumar, Pramod : "Folkicons and Rituals in Tribal Life", Abhinav Publications, 1984, p. 78.
76. Vyas N.N. : A Border Tribe of Rajasthan, Tribe Ed. Vol. IV (1), 1967
77. *Ibid.*, p. 46.
78. Mann, R.S. : Some Aspects of Cultural Life of Damors, Vanyajati (1966), Vol. XIV (2), April, p. 76.
79. *Ibid.*, p. 78.
80 *ibid.*, p. 79.
81. B.J. Dave : Tribe Wartia, (1964), p. 258.
82. Sing, K.S. : People of India, Rajasthan, (1984), Vol. XXXVIII, p. 93.
83. *Ibid.*, p. 98.
84. *Ibid.*, p. 101.
85. Sane, K.J. : "The Wartis", Delhi (1979), p. 74.
86. Kumar, Pramod : Tribe, March (1967), Vol. III, No. 2, p. 37.
87. *Ibid.*, p. 74.
88. Mathur, V.B.: "Folkways in Rajasthan" Himalayan Publication, 1986, p. 91.
89. Census (1991).
90. Das, S.T.: "Lifestyle of Indian Tribal", Grain Publishing House, New Delhi, (1989), Vol. III, p. 272.

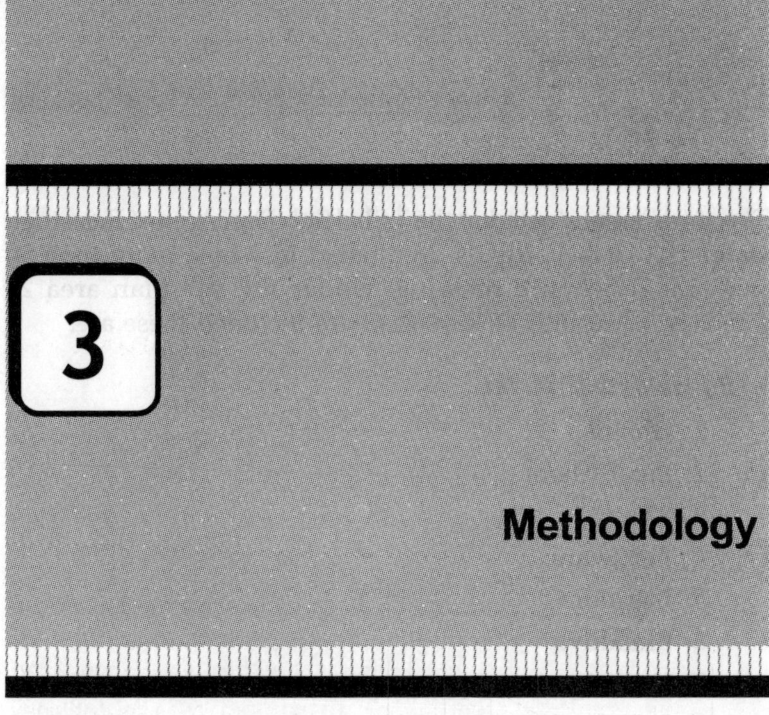

3 Methodology

This chapter deals with the methodology adopted for carrying out the present study. The methodological details of the study are organized under following heads:

1. Locale of the study
2. Selection of villages
3. Selection of sample
4. Development of research tool
5. Collection of data
6. Analysis of data

The detailed information about changing trends in traditional tribal costumes of men and women is obtained through survey. Secondary sources were also explored to get the desired information. The books, magazines, journals and museums viz. Museum of Bhartiya Lok Kala Mandal, Udaipur and Tribal Research Institute, Rajasthan, Udaipur (a unit for promotion of art and culture).

Locale of Study

The study is conducted in the Tribal Sub Plan Area of Rajasthan state. This area is tribals dominated in which more than 50 per cent tribals are residing. Under the sub plan area 23 Panchayat Samities of Rajasthan are included these are:

I. Banswara District

1. Ghatol
2. Pipal Khoot
3. Ghadi
4. Banswara
5. Bagidora
6. Bhukhiya
7. Kushalgarh
8. Sajjangarh

II. Dungarpur (Total District)

1. Dungarpur
2. Bichiwada
3. Simalwada
4. Aaspur
5. Sagwada

III. Udaipur District

Panchayat Samiti-7

1. Jhadol
2. Kotra
3. Kherwada
4. Sarada
5. Salumber
6. Dhariyawad
7. Girwa—81 Villages only

IV. Chittorgarh District

Panchayat Samiti-2

1. Pratapgarh
2. Arnod

V. Sirohi District

Panchayat Samiti-1

1. Abu Road

Selection of Villages

Samples Selection for Bhil Tribe

For the present study Kotra Panchayat Samiti of Udaipur district is selected purposively as the ratio of Bhil population to the total tribal population is highest in the Panchayat Samiti (Appendix-I). From this the four villages are selected purposively keeping in mind the ease of approach.

These are:

1. Bakariya
2. Mandwa
3. Magawas
4. Jogiwar

Sample Selection for Garasia

The Garasia tribe is mainly found in the Abu Road Tehsil of Sirohi District. The four villages are selected purposively keeping in view the ease of approach.

1. Girwar
2. Pindwara
3. Nichla Garh
4. Upla Garh

Sample Selection for Kathodi

Kathodi resides only in the Jhadol Panchayatt Samiti of Udaipur district. They are less as compared to other tribal groups. They are mainly found near Khed Brahma of Gujarat State border. The four densely populated Kathod tribe villages are selected these are:

1. Daiya
2. Ambasa
3. Ambavi
4. Panerwa

Sample Selection for Damor

Damors are residing in the 35 villages of Simalwada panchayat samiti of Dungarpur district, out of these four villages are randomly selected these are:

1. Bhandari
2. Duka
3. Sadariya
4. Buchriya

Selection of Sample

Stratified random sampling procedure is used to draw the sample from each village. In order to collect the information about the changing trends in traditional costume of Bhil, Garasia, Kathodi and Damor. The sample subjects are selected from three different age groups as given below:

This sampling procedure is followed for every tribe i.e. for Bhil tribe 120 people are interviewed i.e., From 4 villages 30 people from 3 different age groups are contacted. Similar procedure is followed for Garasia, Damor and Kathodi tribes.

As it is said that a person would recall only those incidences or information which has occurred when he/she was 8/10 years of age. The recalling power of every person

Village	Age Group						
	20-30 years		30-50 years		50 years & above		Total
	M	F	M	F	M	F	
1	5	5	5	5	5	5	30
2	5	5	5	5	5	5	3.0
3	5	5	5	5	5	5	30
4	5	5	5	5	5	5	30
Grand Total	20	20	20	20	20	20	120

vary. Thus 70 years and above age person would able to recall nearly 60 years back information regarding the costume worn by them and by their parents similarly the people between 30-50 years of age would easily recall between 20-40 years of age would easily recall between 20-40 years back information while young adult between 20-30 years of age would recall only 10-20 years back information. Hence a clear picture about the traditional costume prevalent at:

1. 40-60 years back
2. 20-40 years back
3. 10-20 years back
4. Existing style of costume worn by three different age groups is obtained.

Hence, it is easy to visualise the traditional costumes of Bhil, Garasia, Kathodi, Damore and Changes which has occurred in the last 6 decades.

Development of Tool

Interview method is used for data collection because majority of the tribals are illiterate. Two separate semi-structured interview schedules are prepared for men and women (Appendix II & III). The schedule was consisted of both close ended and open ended questions based on the following outline.

I. Costume

1. Lower and upper garments, construction details fabrics used.
2. Colour and design preferred for the garments.
3. Decoration of the garments.

II. Coiffure

1. Headress-fabric, design, colour, decoration, mode of wearing.
2. Hairstyles

III. Ornaments

1. Jewellery (worn on different body parts, type of metal used, weight, designs available).
2. Tattooing.

IV. Accessories and Footwear

Keen observation is also done to obtain additional information to support the data collected. Photographs of the traditional and contemporary costumes and ornaments are also taken to study the difference between the traditional and contemporary forms of costumes or we can say the change in the traditional form,

Pre-Testing of the Tool

The developed schedule was presented with 10 per cent of the total non-sample subjects to ensure its feasibility and suitability.

Data Collection

The respondents are personally contacted and interviewed to collect the desired information through personal interview at their residences.

Analysis of Data

Data obtained from the survey was coded, tabulated and expressed in frequency and per centage. Per centage was calculated to find out the detail; of costumes, coiffure and ornaments prevalent among both sexes in their different age groups.

4 Costumes of Bhils and Changing Trend

In the view of objective of the study the findings regarding Bhils have been discussed in detail in as under:

Bhil Costume

1. Bhil Female Costume Upper Garment

Table 4.1 gives a clear picture that majority of the respondents of all the three age groups wear Blouse and *Kanchli* as indicated by their respective per centage in the Table 4.1 i.e. 85 per cent females of the young age group, 65 per cent females of middle and 55 per cent females of old age group preferred blouse. However *Kanchli* is most prevalent

Table 4.1 : Distribution of Bhil Female Respondents using different Upper Garments at Present

Costume	Young N = 20		Middle N = 20		Old N = 20		Total N = 60	
	No.	%	No.	%	No.	%	No.	%
Kanchli	3	15	7	35	9	45	19	31.66
Blouse	17	85	13	65	11	55	11	68.38

among old age group where 45 per cent females of the young age group, 65 per cent females of middle and 55 per cent females of old age group preferred blouse. However *Kanchli* is most prevalent among old age group where 45 per cent female respondents wear it.

On the whole it can be, clearly observed that these days more than 60 per cent of the respondents wear blouse, while *Kanchli* is worn by only 31.66 per cent.

This shift is basically due to the changes that have occured in their life style through wider exposure to different mass media as observed at the time of data collection.

Changing Trend in Female Upper Garments

It was observed that the traditional Bhil female upper garment is *Kanchli.*

Table 4.2 : Trend of Bhil Female upper Garments in last 6 decades

Costume	Young N=20		Middle N=20		Old N=20	
	Last 2 decades		Last 4 decades		Last 6 decades	
	No.	%	No.	%	No.	%
Kanchli	15	75	20	100	20	100
Blouse	5	25	–	–	–	–

The Table 4.2 reveals that according to majority of young respondents. Bhils women wear *kanchli* two decade before. Prior to this *kanchli* is the only upper garment worn by Bhil females as reported by all the respondents of middle and old age group. In other words blouse came into existence only two decade before.

Design Details of Female Upper Garments

(i) Neckline

(*a*) ***Kanchli*** : In the traditional upper garment *kanchli* the pentagonal neckline is still prevalent and no variation is observed.

(b) **Blouse:** In the blouse various shapes of neckline are observed. Most common are round, square, V-shape and pentagonal. The Bhil females of above 50 years of age wear only round neckline in the blouse, while the other neckline shapes are used by the females between 20-40 years of age.

The reason for not having any change in the neckline shape of *kanchli* is due to its special construction technique which results in traditional pentagonal shape On the contrary, blouse is a simpler form of upper garment providing wider scope for adaptation of any style in the neckline area.

(ii) Opening

(a) ***Kanchli:*** For the convenience of wearing an opening is usually made in the upper garment. In the *kanchli* opening is always at the back side. Strings are used as fasteners in *kanchli,* it is tied with four strings at the back with two at the neckline and two at the waistline.

(b) **Blouse:** Opening of the blouse is common in front these days. The different types of fasteners are used in the blouse, some of these are button and button hole, hooks and eyes etc. But during data collection it is observed that majority of the Bhil female wear blouse with Button and Button hold as fasteners.

Kanchli is an age old upper garment having opening at the back, which sometimes creates problem and seems uncomfortable. So, when new upper garment blouse came into vogue with front opening, it is easily adopted by the younger generation.

(iii) Sleeve

(a) ***Kanchli:*** The sleeve used in the *kanchli* is a variation of Raglan sleeve and the length is always upto elbow, No variation in the sleeve length and sleeve style is observed.

(b) ***Blouse:*** Set-in sleeve is the only sleeve style observed in the blouse and its length is also upto elbow. However, in the younger generation the trend of the puff sleeves is also observed. Puffs are seen at shoulder only.

The emergence of puff sleeve in the blouse is a direct example of interaction of tribal Bhil group with non-tribal and impact of modernization. But no variation in the sleeve style and length is observed in the *kanchli* because of its special construction technique.

(iv) Length

(a) ***Kanchli:*** It is a shorter upper garment and its length was always kept just below the bossom. No variation is observed in the length of *Kanchli*.

(b) ***Blouse:*** Blouse length varied from 2" to 4" above the waist line. The old females wear the blouse length 4" above the waistline while the young females wear the length just 2" above the waistline.

Kanchli is a peculiar type of upper garment in which the length is fixed and can not be varied. If changed then the fitting is adversely affected. On the other hand the length of the blouse vary according to the individual taste. The old females wear shorter length blouse because previously they used to wear *Kanchli* which is a shorter upper garment while young females wear comparatively longer length blouse.

Changing Trend in Design Details of Female Upper Garments

The design details of traditional upper garment *Kanchli* includes neckline shape, opening, sleeve style and length of the *Kanchli.* No variation is observed in these design details from last 6 decades till today because of its peculiar specific construction technique.

Fitting Style of the Female Upper Garments

Table 4.3 reveals a clear picture about the fitting style the upper garment on the whole 65 per cent of the female respondents wear fitted upper garment 20 per cent semifitted and 15 per cent preferred loose upper garment. Further majority of young Bhil females (90%) wear fitted upper garment and only 10 per cent wear semifitted. The loose upper garment worn maximum by old age group females, while it is totally absent in the younger group. *Kanchli* which is a traditional Bhil female upper garment and is always worn fitted.

Table 4.3: Distribution of Bhil Female Respondents for Fitting Style of the Upper Garments used at Present

Fitting Style	Young N=20		Middle N=20		Old N=20		Total N=60	
	No.	%	No.	%	No.	%	No.	%
Fitted	18	90	12	60	9	45	39	65
Semi fitted	2	10	7	35	3	15	12	20
Loose	–	–	1	5	8	40	9	15

During data collection it was observed that the young Bhil female are very much concerned about fitting of their upper garment. As proper fitting of the garment improves the personality of the wearer.

Use of Readymade, Tailormade and Homemade upper Garments

Table 4.4 Reveals that none of the respondents use homemade upper garments out of the three age group, while readymade are only used by young age group females (25%). In the middle and old age groups cent per cent respondents are tailormade upper garments, thus it can be concluded that the tailormade garment (91.66%) wore most popular among the Bhil females.

Bhil females do not know the stitching of such complicated garments they wore i.e. *Kanchli* and blouse, although they should do some repairing at home by hand stitching. Besides this various sizes of *blouse/Kanchli* are not available in readymade forms. These two may be the vital reasons of wearing and also preferring tailormade garments.

Table 4.4: Distribution of Bhil Female Respondents for the Use of Readymade, Tailormade and Homemade upper Garments at Present

Particulars	Young N=20		Middle N=20		Old N=20		Total N=60	
	No.	%	No.	%	No.	%	No.	%
Readymade	5	25	-	-	-	-	5	8.33
Tailormade	15	75	20	100	20	100	55	91.66
Homemade	-	-	-	-	-	-	-	-

Changing Trend in use of Readymade, Tailormade and Homemade Upper Garments

Table 4.5 clearly reveals that readymade garments are not used during last six decades as reported by the respondents. Where as tailormade garments are popular from last two decades however they are not used by majority four decades before. While 40 per cent respondents started using tailormade garment from last 4 decades. This trend was reverse in case of home made upper garment i.e. majority of

Table 4.5: Trend in use of Readymade, Tailor made and Homemade upper Garments in last 6 decades by Bhil Women

Costume	Young N=20		Middle N=20		Old N=20	
	Last 2 decades		Last 4 decades		Last 6 decades	
	No.	%	No.	%	No.	%
Readymade	-	-	-	-	-	-
Tailormade	16	80	8	40	5	25
Homemade	4	20	12	60	15	75

the respondents (60-75%) use home made garments before 4 decades while the use of home made garments was decreased from last 2 decade. Thus it can be concluded that the use of tailormade upper garment is increasing with the passage of time while the use of homemade is decreasing and today it is totally absent.

Fabric Details

(i) Type of Fabric available and Preferred for Upper Garment

Cotton and synthetic are the two fabrics that are abundantly available in the local market. But the preference for the fabric vary according to the age group as shown in Table 4.6.

Table 4.6 : Distribution of Bhil Female Respondents regarding Fabric Preference for Upper Garment used at Present

Fabric	Young N=20		Middle N=20		Old N=20		Total N=60	
	No.	%	No.	%	No.	%	No.	%
Cotton	-	-	4	20	7	35	11	18.33
Synthetic	20	100	16	80	13	65	49	81.66

Findings of the Table 4.6 highlighted the fact that today about 81.66 per cent females are using synthetic fabrics for upper garments, while remaining 18.33 per cent respondents use only cotton. The females of young age group preferred only synthetic fabric, while in other two age groups preference for both the fabrics are observed.

The inclination towards synthetic fabric is increased because it is more durable, require less care and maintenance, easy to wash and moreover colours are also fast to laundry.

(ii) Colours choice in Upper Garments

In response to the colour preferences in the upper garments it is found that Bhil females were very fond of bright and colourful dresses as they prefer red, yellow, orange and other fluorescent colours. This statement is also supported by Bhanawat (1992) who concluded from his study that Bhil prefer women colourful dress.

They had no restriction of wearing any colour except black. The black is worn by widows only but some young females did not follow this restriction. The females wear contrast colour upper garment with *ghaghra* and *odhni*. They prefer dark colours viz. red, yellow, orange, dark blue, green, fluorescent yellow and orange, purple, etc.

(iii) Fabric prints of Upper Garments

The Table 4.7 reveals that the respondents of all the three age groups used to wear plain fabric over printed fabric for their upper garment as indicated by their percentage i.e. 55 per cent females of the young age group and 80 per cent females of both middle and old age groups. However Printed fabrics are most prevalent in young age group where 45 per cent of the female respondents were using printed fabrics for upper garment.

Table 4.7: Distribution of Bhil Female Respondents for Fabric Prints in Upper Garments used at Present

Fabric Print	Young N=20		Middle N=20		Old N=20		Total N=60	
	No.	%	No.	%	No.	%	No.	%
Plain	11	55	16	80	16	80	43	71.66
Printed	9	45	4	20	4	20	17	28.33

On an average, it can be observed that more than 70 per cent of the respondents wear plain fabric upper garment, while printed are worn only by 28.33 per cent.

The main reason of wearing plain fabric upper garment is that it frequently matches and contrast with different printed lower garments and thus reduces the necessity of purchasing a separate *blouse/Kanchli* with every *ghaghra*.

Changing Trend in Fabric Details

(i) Type of fabric available and preferred for upper garments

The Table 4.8 reveals the fact that synthetic fabric is available in the local market from last 2 decade only as said by the younger group and prior to this cotton fabric is available as reported by middle and old age females.

Table 4.8 : Trend of Fabric Preference by Bhil Female for Upper Garment in last 6 Decades

Fabric	Young N=20		Middle N=20		Old N=20	
	Last 2 decades		Last 4 decades		Last 6 decades	
	No.	%	No.	%	No.	%
Cotton	4	20	20	100	20	100
Synthetic	16	80	–	–	–	–

With the emergence of synthetic fabric the preference for synthetic fabric increased and today maximum Bhil females are using synthetic fabric for their upper garment.

(ii) Colour Choice in Upper Garments

All the bright colours that are available in the local market are worn by Bhil females and they had no restriction of wearing any colour as reported by the respondents.

(iii) Fabric Prints of Upper Garments

Table 4.9 reveals that 80 per cent female of the old age group were using printed fabrics since last 6 decades, while younger group female were using plain garments since a decade back.

Table 4.9: Trend of Fabric Print in Bhil Female Upper Garments from Last 6 Decades

Fabric Print	Young N=20		Middle N=20		Total N=60	
	Last 2 decades		Last 4 decades		Last 6 decades	
	No.	%	No.	%	No.	%
Plain	10	50	7	35	4	20
Printed	10	50	13	65	16	80

Thus from Table 4.7 and Table 4.9 it can be summarized that 6 decades back printed fabrics are in vogue but with the passage of time the use of plain fabric increased over printed fabrics.

Decoration of Upper Garment

As such no decoration is done on the upper garments. Sometimes the '*Kore*' is stitched on the sleeves of *blouse/Kanchli* to make it shiny and attractive. Kore is like a satin ribbon of 1 cm width and it is of either golden or silver colour.

Traditionally also this *kore* is used. At that time no other type of decoration is prevalent.

Ceremonial Upper Garment

The Bhil females have no separate ceremonial upper garment. On the occasion they wear their good conditioned upper garment and sometimes when they have some money they purchase new upper garment, but it is similar to their style of casual wear upper garment. Similar reporting are made by all the respondents regarding ceremonial upper garments wear during last 2-6 decades.

At the time of data collection it was observed that the economic conditions of the tribals are poor. This is the main reason which adversely affect the purchasing power of these people.

This is in concurrence with the findings of Mann (1978) who in his study reported that the economic has led many of the Bhils to work under a system of bonded labour of which not only they but the members of their families are pledged to render service to redeem their debts.

II. LOWER GARMENT

The female lower garment is basically of three styles. They were *Gherdar Ghaghra,* Pleated *ghaghra* and Petticoat.

Table 4.10: Distribution of Bhil Female Respondent using different Lower Garments

Costume	Young N=20		Middle N=20		Old N=20		Total N=60	
	No.	%	No.	%	No.	%	No.	%
Gherdar Ghaghra	4	20	8	40	17	85	29	48.33
Pleated Ghaghra	8	40	10	50	3	15	21	35
Petticoat	8	40	2	10	–	–	10	16.66

Table 4.10 reveals the fact that on the whole about 50 per cent Bhil females wear *gherdar ghaghra* followed by pleated *ghaghra* (35%) and petticoat *ghaghra* (16.66%).

Here it is interesting to note that petticoat *ghaghra* is maximum worn by young age group, while majority of old age group female wear *gherdar ghaghra.*

The changes in the style of *ghaghra* is direct indication of impact of urban areas on the tribal people. The petticoat wear by young Bhil females seems to be an adaptation of petticoat which is most common lower garment worn by urban females under saree. However old females still wear their traditional *Ghaghra* without any variation.

Changing Trend in Females Lower Garments

The *gherdar ghaghra* is the traditional Bhil female lower garment.

Table 4.11: Trend of Bhil Female Lower Garments in last 6 Decades

Costume	Young N=20		Middle N=20		Old N=20	
	Last 2 decades		Last 4 decades		Last 6 decades	
	No.	%	No.	%	No.	%
Gherdar Ghaghra	15	75	20	100	20	100
Pleated Ghaghra	5	25	-	-	-	-

The data furnished in Table 4.11 reveals that between last 2-6 decade only *gherdar ghaghra* was worn by Bhil female as reported by middle and old age group females and *pleated ghaghra* was used from last 1 decade by a few respondents of younger group (25%).

The Table 4.10 and Table 4.11 also reveals that between last 6 decade only *gherdar ghaghra* was known but iri last 1 decades a new pleated *ghaghra* was also worn by Bhil females. A third style in the lower garment i.e. Petticoat *ghaghra* was emerged only recently.

Design Details of Lower Garment

(i) Length

(a) ***Gherdar ghaghra :*** The length of the *gherdar ghaghra* is three fourth i.e. between knee and ankle.

(b) ***Pleated ghaghra:*** The length of this *ghaghra* is full i.e. upto ankle.

(c) ***Petticoat Ghaghra:*** The length of Petticoat is also full i.e. upto ankle.

The reason for having 3/4 length of the *gherdar ghaghra* is to show *pinjani,* (an ornament worn in the legs from ankle to mid of the calf) by these Bhil females. The other two lower garments were emerged only one decade back and from this time they had stop wearing such a wide *'Pinjani* and hence preferred full length *ghaghra.*

(ii) Fabric Requirement

(a) ***Gherdar Ghaghra:*** It is a gathered one and required about 5 to 10 meter fabric for making gher (width of the *ghaghra)* and 2 meter contrast colour fabric for putting *magzi* at hemline and for waistbelt.

(b) ***Pleated Ghaghra:*** The fabric required for this type *of ghaghra* was about 3 meter.

(c) ***Petticoat:*** Two or two and half meter fabric is required for petticoat. In petticoat at the bottom a wide embroidered panel is attached and *ghaghra* is always of plain fabric.

'Gherdar ghaghra' the name itself indicates that the fabric requirement is more to prepare gher (width of the fabric). The total fabiic required is 7 to 12 m. As the requirement of gher reduces the fabric requirement also reduce. Petticoat which is somewhat similar to the petticoat wear under saree required only 2 to $2^1/_2$ meter fabric. However in pleated *ghaghra,* knife pleats are made and therefore the fabric requirement is directly proportional to the width of pleat and waist size.

Changing Trend in Design Details of Lower Garments

No changes are reported by the respondents regarding the design detail of *gherdar ghaghra* since last 4 decades till today.

Use of Reach made, Tailormade and Home made Lower Garments

Table 4.12 highlighted the fact that none of the respondent preferred homemade lower garments. Out of the three age groups old females use only tailormade lower garments, while respondents to other age groups wear tailormade as well as readymade lower garments.

Table 4.12 : Distribution of Bhil Female Respondents for the use of Readmade, Tailormade and Homemade Lower Garments used at Present

Particulars	Young N=20		Middle N=20		Old N=20		Total N=60	
	No.	%	No.	%	No.	%	No.	%
Readymade	8	40	4	0	–	–	12	20
Tailormade	12	60	16	80	20	100	48	80
Homemade	–	–	–	–	–	–	–	–

On the whole it can be seen that 80 per cent females wear tailormade lower garment and only 20 per cent wear readymade.

Changing Trend in use of Readymade, Tailormade and Homemade Lower Garments

A glance at Table 4.13 clarifies that according the old age group females, 6 decade back both tailormade and homemade garments are used, but with the passage of time preference for homemade was decreased upto 5 per cent, in last 4 decades on the other hand the use of tailormade was increased upto 95 per cent, a decade back as reported by younger group.

Table 4.13 : Trend of Bhil Female in use of Readymade, Tailormade and Homemade lower Garments during last 6 decades

Costume	Young N=20		Middle N=20		Old N=20	
	Last 2 decades		Last 4 decades		Last 6 decades	
	No.	%	No.	%	No.	%
Readymade	-	-	–	-	-	-
Tailormade	19	95	13	65	10	50
Homemade	1	5	7	35	10	50

Findings of Table 4.12 and Table 4.13 clarifies that tailormade *ghagfrra* is the most preferred style since last 6 decades till today no readymade *ghaghra* were are between last 2-6 decades, while today no homemade *ghaghra* are used.

Fabric Details

Regarding fabric and colour used in lower graments the findings are similar to that of upper garment.

(i) Type of Fabric Available and Preferred for Lower Garment

For lower garments also cotton and synthetic are the two fabrics that are largely available in the local market, but the preference for a particular fabric vary according to the age group as shown in Table 4.14.

Table 4.14 : Distributions of Bhil female respondents for present fabric preference for lower garments

Fabric	Young N=20		Middle N=20		Old N=20		Total N=60	
	No.	%	No.	%	No.	%	No.	%
Cotton	–	–	4	20	6	30	10	16.66
Synthetic	20	100	16	80	14	70	50	83.33

The Table 4.14 reveals that for lower garments synthetic fabrics are most preferred. This is supported by Vijayanand (2000) who concluded from his study that synthetic fabrichave become very much popular because they have certain desirable properties. These properties are high strength, wash and wear property, good dimensional stability and elegant appearance.

(ii) Colours Preferences

In response to the colour preference in lower garment it was found that they had no restriction of wearing any colour in lower garment but black, white, brown and grey colours are not worn by these females. They prefer only bright colours viz. such as yellow, orange, red, maharoon, blue, etc.

(iii) Fabric Print of Lower Garment

The Table 4.15 reveals the fact that on the whole 76.66 per cent Bhil females wear printed *ghaghra* and only 23.33 per cent wear plain *ghaghra.* In the young age group plain and printed *ghaghra* are equally worn while in middle and old age group the percentage of use of printed fabirc is more i.e. 80 per cent and 85 per cent respectively.

Table 4.15: Distribution of Bhil Female Respondents for Fabric Print of lower Garments used at Present

Fabric	Young N=20		Middle N=20		Old N=20		Total N=60	
	No.	%	No.	%	No.	%	No.	%
Plain	10	50	4	20	3	15	7	23.33
Printed	10	50	16	80	7	85	43	76.66

The different types of prints are available in the fabric but the most common is floral print for the *ghaghra.* The plain fabric are generally used in the petticoat, because embroidery can be, done on it.

Changing Trend in Fabirc Details

For *ghaghra* only cotton fabric is available in the Bhil market between 2-6 decades. Today synthetic fabrics are available therefore preference for synthetic fabric increases over cotton.

Table 4.16 gives a clear picture that in 2-6 decade printed fabrics are used for lower garments why majority of respondents of all age group (75-100%).

However use of plain fabric for lower garments has been started from last 2 decades as reported by a few young respondents (25%).

Table 4.16: Changing Trend in Fabrics Print of Bhil Lower Garment

Fabric Plain	Young N=20		Middle N=20		Old N=20	
	Last 2 decades		Last 4 decades		Last 6 decades	
	No.	%	No.	%	No.	%
Plain	5	25	2	10	–	–
Printed	15	75	18	90	20	100

Decoration used for Lower Garment

As such no decoration is done on the *gherdar ghaghra* and pleated *ghaghra,* but petticoat are decorated with the machine embroidery. The coloured embroidery threads are used for embroidery. The motifs are usually leaves, flowers and some time very small birds etc. Traditionally no decoration is done on the *ghaghra.*

Ceremonial Lower Garment

On the ceremonial occasions only *gherdar ghaghra* is worn as a lower garment by the females. As it is their traditional *ghaghra.*

III. COIFFURE

Head-dress

During the field visit it is observed that *odhni* is the only head-dress worn by the Bhil females by all the three age groups though the dimensions of the head-dress vary according to the age group and also by individual choice.

Table 4.17 : Different Types of Bhil *odhni*

Odhni	Length	Width
I style	$2^1/_2$ m	$1^1/_2$ m
II style	$1^1/_2$ m	1 m

Table 4.18 : Distribution of Bhil Female Respondents for Dimensions of Headdress use at Present

Dimension	Young N=20		Middle N=20		Old N=20		Total N=60	
	No.	%	No.	%	No.	%	No.	%
$1^1/_2$ by $2^1/_2$ m	17	85	12	60	9	45	38	63.33
1 m by $1^1/_2$ m	3	15	8	40	11	55	12	36.66

The Table 4.18 reveals fact that on the whole about two third of the Bhil female respondents wear headdress of $1^1/_2$ m by $2^1/_2$ m dimension while only one third respondents wear headdress of 1m by $1^1/_2$ dimension.

Here it is interesting to note that larger size of *odhni* was maximum worn by younger age group, while old age group females wear relatively shorter size.

Style of Wearing Odhni

These two different sizes of *odhni* are wear by two styles. The *odhni* of $1^1/_2$ m by $2^1/_2$ m. dimension is worn in the way that one end of the *odhni* is pleated and tucked into the *ghaghra,* while the other end was taken around the torso, over the head brought to the front to be left loose or tucked in at the waist.

The second style was very different from the previous one. In this style the centre of the odhni is tucked on to the head and both the ends were left open or sometimes tucked into the *ghaghra.*

Changing Trend in Headdress

The *odhni* is the traditional headdress wear by the Bhil females from last 6 decades till today but changes are observed in the dimensions.

It is evident from the Table 4.19 that most of the Bhil females wear odhni of 1 m by $1^1/_2$ m dimension between last 2 to 6 decades as reported by respondents of all the three age group, while larger size odhni is seen from last 4 decades (according to middle age group) but prior to this it is not seen.

Table 4.19: Trend in Dimensions of Headdress worn by Bhil Female from last 6 Decades

Dimensions	Young N=20		Middle N=20		Old N=20	
	Last 2 decades		Last 4 decades		Last 6 decades	
	No.	%	No.	%	No.	%
$1\frac{1}{2}$m by $2\frac{1}{2}$m	4	20	2	10	–	–
1 m by $1\frac{1}{2}$m	16	80	18	90	20	100

The change was observed in the size of the *odhni.* Today larger size is more prevalent than shorter one. While between last 2-6 decades shorter is more prevalent.

The wearing style of the odhni is same as today shorter style *odhni* in which the centre of the odhni is tucked on to be head and both the ends are left open or sometimes tucked into the *ghaghra.*

Fabric Details

(i) Type of fabric available and Preferred

Both cotton and synthetic are largely available in the local market. But the preference for a particular fabric vary according to the age group as shown in Table-20.

Table 4.20: Distribution of Bhil Female Respondents for Fabric Preference for Headdress used or Present

Fabric	Young N=20		Middle N=20		Old N=20		Total N=60	
	No.	%	No.	%	No.	%	No.	%
Cotton	6	30	6	30	7	35	19	31.66
Synthetic	14	70	14	70	13	65	41	68.33

Table-20 highlighted the fact that the respondents of all the three age groups have been given more preference to synthetic fabric over cotton fabric as indicated by 68.33 per cent, while cotton is worn only by 31.66 per cent.

(ii) Colours Preferred

Bhil females wear all the bright colours such as red, yellow, orange, green, purple, magneta, etc.

(iii) Fabric Print of Headdress

Table 4.21: Distribution of Bhil Female Respondents for Fabric Prints in Headdress used at Present

Fabric Print	Young N=20		Middle N=20		Old N=20		Total N=60	
	No.	%	No.	%	No.	%	No.	%
Plain	10	50	14	70	16	80	40	66.66
Printed	10	50	6	30	4	20	20	33.33

The Table 4.21 reveals out the fact that on the whole two third Bhil female respondents wear plain *odhni* and only one third wear printed *odhni.* In the younger age group plain and printed *odhni* are equally preferred, while in middle and old age group the preference for plain fabric is more i.e. 70 and 80 per cent respectively. As plain odhni matches with *vveryghaghra* its preference is more.

Changing Trend in Fabric Details

(i) Type of Fabric Available and Preferred

For odhni only cotton fabric is available in the local market between last 2-6 decades as reported by the female of all the age groups therefore they had no other choice so they wear only cotton *odhni.*

Today both cotton and synthetic are readily available in the market, but they give preference to synthetic fabric than cotton because of its multiple advantages over cotton.

(ii) Colours Preferred

In last 2-6 decades all the colours that are easily available in the market are worn by Bhil females.

(iii) Fabric Print of Headdress

The Table 4.22 reveals the fact that from last 2-6 decade the printed fabrics are worn more than plain fabrics as told by all the three age group females. Mainly Block printed *odhni* were worn by these females.

Table 4.22 : Trend of Fabric Print in Bhil Female Headdress from last 6 Decades

Costume	Young N=20		Middle N=20		Old N=20	
	Last 2 decades		Last 4 decades		Last 6 decades	
	No.	%	No.	%	No.	%
Plain	4	20	4	20	—	—
Printed	16	80	16	80	20	100

Here it is concluded from the Table 4.21 and Table 4.22 that today plain fabrics are used as headdress, while traditionally printed are used.

Ceremonial Headdress

Bhil females generally wear same type of *odhni* as they wear in casual days. But sometimes for occasions they stitch golden or silver Kore on all the four sides of their *odhni* and when it is worn as casual wear the kore is removed.

Similar reporting are made for the of decoration *of odhni* between last 1-6 decades also.

Hair Style

The two hairstyles are prevalent among Bhil females i.e. open hair style and braided style.

Table 4.23: Distribution of Bhil Female Respondents for different Hairstyle used at Present

Hairstyle	Young N=20		Middle N=20		Old N=20		Total N=60	
	No.	%	No.	%	No.	%	No.	%
Open	8	40	4	20	3	15	15	25
Braided	12	60	16	80	17	85	45	75

Table 4.23 reveals the fact that in general about 75 per cent Bhil females kept their hair braided while only 25 per cent kept their hair open. It also point out that most of the respondents of all the three age group kept their hair braided as indicated by their percentages i.e. 60 per cent females of young age group, 80 per cent females of middle and 85 per cent of old age group. The open hair maximum kept by young females (40%).

It was observed that the Bhil females spend a lot of time for caring their hair. Similar reporting was made by Mehta (1993) who reported that Bhil females spend a lot of time to make their hair beautiful. They wash their hair from curd, milk or *multani mini* weekly or fortnightly. Oiling of hair is common among these people.

Hair Cutting

The Table 4.24 reveals the fact that hair cutting is preferred maximum in the young age group (75%), while in middle age

Table 4.24: Distribution of Bhil Female Respondents for Preference of Hair Cutting at Present

Fabric	Young N=20		Middle N=20		Old N=20		Total N=60	
	No.	%	No.	%	No.	%	No.	%
Hair Cutting	15	75	5	25	-	-	20	33.33
No Hair Cutting	5	25	15	75	20	100	40	66.66

group it reduces to 25 per cent and totally absent in old age group. On the whole one third Bhil females preferred hair cutting and two third did not cut their hair.

The Bhil females kept their hair long from the back and cut only front hair, such hairstyle is called *'Sadhana cut*[1]. It was in the concurrence of the study conducted by Mehta (1993) who reported that Bhil females cut their front hair and allow them to rest on the forehead.

Changing Trend in Hairstyle

No difference was observed in the Bhil female hairstyle from today to last 6 decades. The only change occurred is that today young Bhil females preferred to cut their front hair which was totally absent between last 2-6 decade as reported by middle and old age female.

Hair Decoration

Bhil females give extra attention towards their hair decoration specially when they went to market or to the fairs. They are very fond of using bright coloured hairpins also tie ribbon in their braid. Now a days these females also use rubber bands and hair bands of various styles as these are available in the village itself due to the improved transportation facility.

In response to the question asked about the hair cecoration between 1-6 decade similar results are obtained.

IV. ORNAMENTS

Jewellery

Bhil females are very much fond of Jewellery and wear different types of jewellery in different body parts i.e. neck ear, head, waist, ankle, toes and other body parts. The similar observation wear made by Mandal (1998) who reported that Bhil women wear huge ornaments of silver and alloy metals at their neck, ear, arm, wrist, finger, waist, ankle, toes, forehead and nose.

Table 4.25: Jewellery Worn by Bhil Women on different Body Parts

Sl. No.	Body part	Name of Jewellery	Weight of Jewellery
1.	Head	Bor Borla Jhela	10-15 gm 20-30 gm 80-100 gm
2.	Nose	Long Nath Bhavriya	5-10 gm 10-15 gm 10-15 gm
3.	Ear	Dhimna Oganiya Jumar	10-12 gm 12-15 gm 15-25gm
4.	Neck	Hasali Sakhali Madalia Tagli	1-1$^1/_2$ kg 1-1$^1/_2$ kg 30-40 gm $^1/_2$ to 1$^1/_2$ kg
5.	Hand	Bhujband Kakona Tadiyan Gajara Kada Chelkada	60-70 gm 70-100 gm 60-80 gm 100-300 gm 100-300 gm 100-200 gm
6.	Finger	Viti Hathful	5-15 gm 80-120 gm
7.	Waist	Kandora Judo	600-800 gm 80-120 gm
8.	Ankle	Kadala Anwale Pajab Thankle ghughre	300-500 gm 70-80 gm 100-150 gm 80-100 gm
9.	Toe	Bichhia	5-30 gm

The weight of every ornament vary according to individual preference. Only silver metal is used for different ornaments. Very few Bhil females wear white metal ornaments because they can not afford to buy silver ornaments.

Changing Trend in Jewellery

All the jewelleries that are worn today were also put on in last 1-6 decade back but one most important jewellery which is not worn today but deliberately worn in the past. It was *pinjani* as reported by all the respondents. This was worn in the legs from ankle to mid of the calf. 6 decades back it was made up of mud, but with the passage of time the metal *pinjani* took over the place of mud *pinjani*. *Pinjani* was a set of anklets comprises of 3-4 *kada,* 1 or 2 *Nevri* and one *Datedar Nevri.*

Tattooing

Tattooing is a type of body decoration done on different body parts. These are the permanent marks.

Table 4.26: Distribution of Bhil Female Respondents for Preference of Tattooing at Present

Preference for Tattooing	Young N=20		Middle N=20		Old N=20		Total N=60	
	No.	%	No.	%	No.	%	No.	%
Preferred	17	85	19	95	20	100	56	93.33
Not Preferred	3	15	1	5	–	–	4	6.66

Table 4.26 reveals the fact that Bhil females preferred tattooing as indicated by the over all percentage *i.e.* 93.33 per cent. Rejection for tattooing is maximum in young age group (15%).

Thus it can be said that the tattooing is the commonly preferred body decoration. The most common reasons said by old females for being tattooed is that these marks of tattooing were seen in the heaven and if absent then they will not get salvation. But young and middle age group females prefer tattooing because it increases their beauty.

Das (1989) reported that the object of tattooing is said to be this 'After death each individual in asked whether he has been pricked by thorns in the jungle the presentation of these tatto marks is considered as affirmative answer without this they have to be pricked with thorns in after life.

In response to the questions asked about the body parts on which tattooing is done, age of being tattooed and motifs of tattooing it is found that tattooing is mainly done on hand and face but some people who were very fond of tattooing also get it does on legs and neck. In general it is done at the age of 5-8 years though it vary according to individual preference. Young boys and girls preferred tattooing in the fairs for the sake of latest designs. These are permanent marks of green or of blue colour.

The common motifs used in tattooing are scrorpio, birds, snake, floral designs, name of the individual, kul-devta etc. These are made decorative with small all round designs.

Changing Trend in Tattooing

Last 2-6 decade back the full hands are tattooed but today only one or two designs were made on the hands. Today it is generally done on the hand and face but previously it is also done on the neck and legs.

Materials used for Improving Appearance

The Bhil females are very fond of looking beautiful therefore they use various cosmetic material these cosmetic materials are available in the village itself. The commonly used materials are-powder, creme, Nail polish, lipstick, Hair oil, *Kajal, Surma.* The use of cosmetic material is increasing day-by day because of their exposure towards mass media specially 'Movies' The cosmetics are most frequently used by the young Bhil females.

Changing Trend in Material used for Improving Appearance

For the improvement of appearance the Bhil females are using kajal, powder and Hair oil a decade back as reported by young respondents but middle and old age female said that between last 2-6 decades back only hair oil was used by these females.

V. FOOTWEAR

The Bhil females wear chappal and shoes as footwear but both the footwear vary according to age group.

Table 4.27: Distribution of Bhil Female Respondents were different Footwear at Present

Footwear	Young N=20		Middle N=20		Old N=20		Total N=60	
	No.	%	No.	%	No.	%	No.	%
Chappal	17	85	20	100	20	100	57	95
Shoes	3	15	–	–	–	–	3	5

Table 4.27 reveals the fact that on the whole 95 per cent Bhil females wear chappal and only 5 per cent wear shoes as their footwear. The shoes are only worn by young age group female while middle and old age group Bhil females wear only chappal.

As it is observed during field visit that their economic condition is poor so they can not afford to buy shoes which are comparatively costly than chappal.

Changing Trend in Footwear

The table 4.28 reveals that Bhil females remained bare footed between 2-4 decades as reported by 70 per cent respondents of old age group and 35 per cent of the middle age group, however only 15 per cent respondent of the young age group reported the same findings a decade before. Majority of the young respondents reported about the use of chappal by Bhil females.

Table 4.28: Trend of Bhil female Wearing different Footwears from last 6 Decades

Footwear	Young N=20		Middle N=20		Old N=20	
	Last 2 decades		Last 4 decades		Last 6 decades	
	No.	%	No.	%	No.	%
Bare foot	3	15	7	35	14	70
Chappal	17	85	13	65	6	30

Thus it is concluded from Table 4.27 and Table 4.28 that between 2-6 decades some of the females remain bare footed. Then they slowly shifted to chappal, and today maximum Bhil females wear chappal as footwear and few are shifted to shoes. The chappal is made up of rubber material.

Accessories

Today only two accessories are used by the Bhil females these are 'Tokari' and 'Rumal'. The bag i.e. tokari is made up of plastic wire and generally of green and blue in colour and used as purse. The handkerchief i.e. Rumal, these are very colourful and having different designs.

Table 4.29: Distribution of Bhil Female Respondents for the Preference of Accessories Prevalent at Present

Footwear	Young N=20		Middle N=20		Old N=20		Total N=60	
	No.	%	No.	%	No.	%	No.	%
Accessories preferred	15	75	9	45	8	40	32	53.33
Accessories not preferred	5	25	11	55	12	60	28	46.66

Table 4.29 reveals that on the whole accessories are preferred by about 50 per cent females while remaining 50 per cent are not using any accessory. Here it is interesting

to note that accessories are maximum used by young age group females followed by middle and old as shown by their percentages i.e. 75 per cent, 45 per cent and 40 per cent respectively.

Changing Trend in Accessories

Middle and old age group respondents reported that between 2-6 decades no accessories are used by Bhil females, but younger group said that *'Tokari'* is used as accessory by some of the Bhil females a decades before.

BHIL MALE COSTUME

Upper Garment

The two different types of upper garments commonly worn by Bhil males are *Kurta* and Shirt.

Table 4.30: Distribution of Bhil Male Respondents for Upper Garments used at Present

Costume	Young N=20		Middle N=20		Old N=20		Total N=60	
	No.	%	No.	%	No.	%	No.	%
Kurta	8	40	13	65	20	100	41	68.33
Shirt	12	60	7	35	–	–	19	31.66

Table 4.30 The reveals that the respondents of middle and old age group give more preference to *kurta* over shirt as indicated by their respective per centages in Table 4.30 i.e. 65 per cent of middle age group and cent per cent of old age group. However shirt is more prevalent among young age group where 60 per cent of male respondents prefer it.

On the whole it can be clearly observed that nearly 70 per cent respondents wear *kurta,* while shirt is worn by only 31.66 per cent. From this it is observed that the old males are still more inclined to their traditional costume i.e. *Kurta* as compare to Shirt which is generally worn by younger age group.

Changing Tend in Upper Garment

Kurta is the traditional upper garment of Bhil Males.

Table 4.31: Trend of Bhil Male Upper Garments from last 6 Decades

Costume	Young N=20		Middle N=20		Old N=20	
	Last 2 decades		Last 4 decades		Last 6 decades	
	No.	%	No.	%	No.	%
Kurta	7	35	20	100	20	100
Shirt	13	65	–	–	–	–

The Table 4.31 reveals that according to middle and old age respondents, Bhil male wear only *Kurta* between 2-6 decades, while young respondents reported that shirt is also worn by Bhil males a decade before. In other words shirt came into existence only a decade before.

Design Details of Upper Garment

(i) Neckline

Kurta: The round neckline with or without stand cellar is commonly reported.

Shirt: The standard shirt collar is observed in the shirt.

(ii) Opening

Kurta: In the kurta opening is always in the front and the opening length is about 7" to 9". The opening is finished by placket having button and buttonhole as fasteners.

Shirt: Shirt is fully open from front and button and buttonhole are used as fasteners.

(iii) Sleeve

Plain sleeve is observed in the *kurta* as well as in the shirt. However the sleeve length may vary upto elbow or full length sleeve.

The shirt's full length sleeve is always finished with cuff.

(iv) Length

The length of both *kurta* and shirt is usually upto the hip level which is considered as standard length of the shirt.

Changing Trend in Design Details

The changing trend regarding the design details of the *kurta* between 1-6 decade it is observed that no change is found in the neckline shape, placket opening, sleeve style and length of the *kurta.*

Fitting of the Upper Garment

Regarding fitting of the shirt and *kurta* it is observed that only the standard amount of ease is kept in both the types depending upon the size and shape of the body.

As such no variation is reported by any respondent regarding the fitting style to *kurta* between to 2-6 decade.

Use of Readymade, Tailormade and Homemade upper Garments

The Table 4.32 reveals a clear picture that none of the respondent use homemade upper garment out of the three age group, while readymade are used by younger and middle age group cent per cent respondents wear tailormade upper

Table 4.32: Distribution of Bhil Male Respondents for the Use of Readymade, Tailormade and Homemade upper Garments at Present

Particulars	Young N=20		Middle N=20		Old N=20		Total N=60	
	No.	%	No.	%	No.	%	No.	%
Readymade	4	20	2	10	–	–	6	10
Tailormade	16	80	18	90	20	100	54	90
Homemade	–	–	–	–	–	–	–	–

garment. Thus on the whole it can be said that the tailormade garments (90%) are mostly preferred by Bhil males.

Changing Trend in Use of Readymade Tailor made and Homemade Upper Garments

The Table 4.33 reveals the fact that according to the respondents of all the three age groups, majority of the Bhil men wear tailormade upper garments between last 2-6 decades.

Table 4.33 : Trend of use of Readymade, Tailormade and Homemade upper Garments by Bhil Male from last 6 Decades

Particulars	Young N=20		Middle N=20		Old N=20	
	Last 2 decades		Last 4 decades		Last 6 decades	
	No.	%	No.	%	No.	%
Readymade	–	–	–	–	–	–
Tailormade	20	100	20	100	15	75
Homemade	–	–	–	–	5	25

Hence it can be summarized from Table 4.32 and Table 4.33 that tailormade upper garments are mostly used by Bhil males from last 6 decades. It is also interesting to note that home made garments are becoming out of the sense between 2-6 decades, on the other hand readymade came into the market recently.

Fabric Details

(i) Type of fabric Available and preferred for upper garment

Both cotton and synthetic fabric are abundantly available in the local market. But the preference for the fabric vary according to the age group as shown in Table 4.34.

Table 4.34: Distribution of Bhil male respondents for present fabric preference for upper garments

Fabric	Young N=20		Middle N=20		Old N=20		Total N=60	
	No.	%	No.	%	No.	%	No.	%
Cotton	–	–	3	15	5	25	8	13.33
Synthetic	20	100	17	85	5	75	52	86.33

The Table-34 reveals the fact that today about 86.66 per cent males prefer synthetic fabric for upper garment, while remaining 13.3 per cent respondents prefer cotton. The males of younger age group prefer only synthetic fabric, while in other two age groups the preference for both the fabric are observed.

(ii) Colours preferred in the upper Garment

In response to the colour preferences in the upper garment it is found that Bhil males wear only white colour *kurta,* while shirt is worn of different colours. They prefer bright colours in their shirts, such as red, yellow, orange, green, etc.

(iii) Fabric Print of Upper Garment

The two types of fabric are available in the market for Bhil male upper garment these are plain and printed. The plain white fabric is used for *kurta* and printed for shirt. In the printed fabric various prints are available most common are birds, flowers and geometrical prints.

The main reason of wearing white plain *kurta* is that it matches with the white *dhoti.*

Changing Trend in Fabric Details

The changing trend regarding this feature is observed between last 2-6 decade the only plain white cotton fabric is used for *kurta.*

Ceremonial Upper Garment

The Bhil male did not wear any specific ceremonial dress.

Changing Trend in Ceremonial Upper Garment

Between 2-6 decades back the Bhil males wore *'Gotdar Angi'* which is similar in cut to the *'Bakhatri'* of Gaduliya Lohars, It was made of course unbleached cotton. It has full sleeved hip length garment and double breasted front with a yoke and fasteners at the shoulder and at the centre front. The *Angi* had slits on the sides which were finished with a bias edging. This bias edging also extends to the neck, centre front and hemline. The bias edging was known as the *'Got'* hence the name *'Gotdar Angi'*, A contrast coloured *Got* was used on the *angi*.

Front last 1 decade no special dress is worn on ceremonial occasions but prior to this ' *Gotdar Angi* was worn.

II. LOWER GARMENT

Bhil males wear two types of lower garments i.e. *Dhoti* and *Pant* (trouser).

Table 4.35: Distribution of Bhil male respondents for lower garments used at present

Costume	Young N=20		Middle N=20		Old N=20		Total N=60	
	No.	%	No.	%	No.	%	No.	%
Dhoti	8	40	13	65	20	100	41	68.33
Pant	12	60	7	35	–	–	19	31.66

The Table 4.35 reveals the fact that the respondents of middle and old age group use to wear *Dhoti* than pant as indicated by their percentages i.e. 65 per cent and cent per cent respectively. However pant is worn by younger gioup, where 60 per cent of the male respondents wear it.

On an average it can be observed that more than 65 per cent respondents wear *Dhoti* while only 31.6 per cent wear pant as their lower garment. Gamar (1994) also reported that the Bhils of Rajasthan wear *dhoti.*

Changing Trend in Lower Garment

Dhoti is the traditional lower garment of Bhil males. The details are given below :

Table 4.36 : Changing trend of Bhil male Upper Garments from last 6 decades

Costume	Young N=20		Middle N=20		Old N=20	
	Last 2 decades		Last 4 decades		Last 6 decades	
	No.	%	No.	%	No.	%
Dhoti	17	85	20	100	20	100
Pant	3	15	–	–	–	–

The Table 4.36 reveals that according to majority of the young respondents, Bhil man wear *dhoti* two decade before. Prior to this *dhoti* was the only lower garment worn by Bhil males as reported by all the respondents of middle and old age group. In other words pant came into existence only two decade before.

Design Details of Lower Garment

(i) Length

Both the lower garments i.e. Pant and *Dhoti* are of full length. Short length *Dhoti* (upto knee) is also worn while working. The reason for wearing short length dhoti is to prevent its hinderance while working.

(ii) Fabric Requirement

Dhoti-4 meter long and 1 meter wide fabric is required for *Dhoti.* This is worn by knotting around the waist and the entire length is drawn between the legs and tucked at the back. The *dhoti* is of ankle length and shortened to knee, while working and thus it looks like a pair of close fitted trousers.

Pant-The fabric required for normal height (5′6" to 5′8") individual is 1 meter and 20 cm. The fabric requirement vary according to the height of the individual.

Changing Trend in Design Details of Lower Garments

No Change is observed regarding the length and fabric requirement of *dhoti* between last 2-6 decades.

Preference for Readymade, Tailormade and Homemade Lower Garments

Dhoti is a plain white fabric which is easily and readily available in the market therefore brought readymade. On the other hand tailormade and readymade pants are equally preferred by them.

Fabric Details

(i) Type of fabric available and preferred for lower garments

For lower garment both cotton and synthetic fabrics are largely available in the Bhil market. But the preference for particular fabric vary according to the age group as shown in Table 4.37.

Table 4.37: Distribution of Bhil male Respondents for Present Fabric Preference for Lower Garments

Fabric	Young N=20		Middle N=20		Old N=20		Total N=60	
	No.	%	No.	%	No.	%	No.	%
Cotton	-	-	7	35	10	50	17	28.33
Synthetic	20	100	13	65	10	50	43	71.66

The Table 4.37 reveals that on the whole synthetic fabric is more preferred than cotton fabric for lower garment.

(ii) Colour Preference and Fabric Print

In response to the colour preference in the lower garment it is found that Bhil males wear only white colour in *dhoti* and it pant the darker shades are more preferred printed fabric were not at all worn by them.

Changing Trend in Fabric Details

Between 2-6 decades the plain white cotton *dhoti* is worm by Bhils as said by middle and old age group males, on the other hand younger group reported that a decade back synthetic plain white *dhoti* is also worn by Bhil male.

III. COIFFURE

1. Headdress

During field visit it was found that *Pagadi* (turban) is the only headdress worn by the Bhil males.

Table 4.38 : Distribution of Bhil male Respondents for Preference of Headdress at Present

Particulars	Young N=20		Middle N=20		Old N=20		Total N=60	
	No.	%	No.	%	No.	%	No.	%
Preferred	3	15	8	40	16	80	27	45
Not Preferred	17	85	12	60	4	20	33	55

The Table 4.38 reveals that in general it is worn by nearly half of the respondents while remaining respondents does not prefer any headdress. From all the three age groups *pagadi* is maximum worn by old age group (80%), while it is minimum worn by young age group males (15%).

The middle and old aged males reported that traditional i.e. between 2-6 decades every Bhil male *wear pagadi* as headdress and the rejection *for pagadi* is started from last 2 decade only.

Thus it can be said that the traditional style of wearing headdress is slowly decreasing. Similar results are obtained by Lokhit Vikas Sansthan (1989) who found that the persons belonging to new generation do not wear any, headdress.

Dimension and Mode of Wearing the Headdress

Only one dimension of *pagadi* is prevalent among Bhil males i.e. 5.5 mt. long and 16″ wide. The *pagadi* is worn in a particular style the fabric is first twisted then it is draped around the head three times, now its direction was reversed and one more turn was taksn and the remaining fabric was tucked at the back.

According to all the male respondents the same dimensions and mode of wearing of *pagadi* is prevalent between last 6 decades.

Fabric Details

The plain and printed cotton readymade fabric is used for *pagadi*. During the field visit it was observed that Bhil males are very fond of wearing bright colours *pagadi*. Some frequently worn colours are red, yellow, orange and many times they also use white *pagadi*.

Bhils males wear plain *pagadi* i.e. without any decoration. They had no separate headdress for ceremonial, the same causal wear headdress is worn on occasion.

The similar reporting are made by males of all age groups for last 2-6 decades regarding fabric details decoration and ceremonial *pagadi*.

2. Hairstyle

No special hairstyle is observed among the Bhil males. They comb their hair with or without partition depends upon the size of the hair. If hair are cut short then combing is done without partition but if these are long then parted from the middle and then combed. They generally went for frequent hair cutting once or even twice in a month. *Hairoil* is used by these people in order to make their hair shiny.

Changing Trend in Hairstyle

Six decades back Bhil male kept their hair long without combing and hair cutting is done once in one or two years as reported by the older group, while middle age group males said that from last 2-6 decades the frequency of hair cutting is increased i.e. once in six or seven months and combing of hair is also started While a decade back the partition and regular hair combing is started and they also went for frequent hair cutting i.e. once in a month.

Thus it can be concluded that in the past Bhil males kept their hair long and the length of hair reduced with the passage of time and today they kept very short hair. The frequency of hair cutting was also increased i.e. it was once or twice in last 6 decades now it is increased up to once or even twice in a month.

Ornaments

1. Jewellery

Bhil Males are also fond of jewellery and wear different types

Table 4.39 : Jewellery Worn on Different Body parts with Their Weight by Bhil Males

Sl. No.	Body part	Name of Jewellery	Weight of Jewellery
1.	Ear	Murki	5-10 gm
2.	Neck	Sakhali Tagli	$1\text{-}1^1/_2$ kg $^1/_2\text{-}1^1/_2$ kg
3.	Hand	Kade	30-40 gm
4.	Finger	Character	5-25 gm
5.	Waist	Kandora	600-800 gm
6.	Ankle	Kadala	300-500 gm

of jewellery in different body parts i.e. neck, ear, ankle, waist. The similar observation are made by Mathur (1986) who reported that the Bhil men in wagged region are extremely fond of ornaments. They wear *Jhela* and *Murki* in their earlobes, *Kada* of gold or silver on their wrist, *Beenthi* (Ring) on the fingers and *Anklets* on the right beg as a mark of social distinction.

The weight of every ornament vary according individual preference.

Metal Used

Only silver metal is used for different ornaments. Very few Bhil males wear white metal ornaments because they did not afford to buy silver ornaments.

Changing Trend in Jewellery

Bhil males wear the same jewellery between last 2-6 decades as they wear today. Thus it can be summarized that traditional and contemporary jewellery of Bhil males are similar and no change had been observed from last 6 decades.

Tattooing

The Table 4.40 reveals the fact that majority of the Bhil males preferred tattooing as indicated by their overall percentage

Table 4.40 : Distribution of Bhil Male Respondents for Preference of Tattooing at Present

Tattooing	Young N=20		Middle N=20		Old N=20	
	Last 2 decades		Last 4 decades		Last 6 decades	
	No.	%	No.	%	No.	%
Preferred	18	90	20	100	58	96.66
Not Preferred	2	10	-	-	2	3.33

i.e. 96.66 per cent (Rejection for tattooing is only observed in the young age group which is very less.

Thus it is said that the tattooing is the commonly preferred body decoration. The most common reason said by the old males for being tattooed is that these marks of tattooing shows their social status in the society.

During the field visit it is observed that tattooing is mainly done on hands. In general it is done at the age of 5-8 years though it vary according to individual preference. Your boys preferred to be tattooed in the fairs for latest designs.

Changing Trend in Tattooing

Traditional and contemporary tattooing are very much similar, the only difference lies in the amount of tattooing as reported by the Bhil males that between 2-6 decades full hands are tattooed but today only one or two designs are made on the hand.

Materials used for Improving Appearance

The Bhil males are also very fond of looking handsome so they use various cosmetic materials for improving their appearance. These materials are available in the local market.

The use of cosmetic materials is increasing day-by-day because of their exposure towards mass-media specially 'Movies' and these are frequently used by the yoimg Bhil males.

Changing Trend in Material Used for Improving Appearance

Two to six decades back only hair oil is used by Bhil males as reported by young and middle age group respondents. But prior to this nothing is used for improving the appearance as said by old people.

Thus it can be summarized that 6 decades back Bhil males are not giving any attention towards improving their appearance. But after that the interest is developed for improving the appearance so different materials are used for it.

Footwear

The Table 4.41 highlight the fact that on the whole almost equal number of respondents wear chappal and *mojadia* i.e. 38.33 per cent and 41.66 per cent respectively and only 20 per cent respondents wear shoes. It also shows that *Mojadia* are maximum worn by old age group males, and shoes are mostly worn by young and middle aged Bhil males.

Table 4.41: Distribution of Bhil male Respondents were different Footwears at Present

Footwear	Young N=20		Middle N=20		Old N=20		Total N=60	
	No.	%	No.	%	No.	%	No.	%
Chappal	9	45	9	45	5	25	23	38.33
Shoes	8	40	4	20	–	–	12	20
Mojadia	3	15	7	35	15	75	25	41.66

Respondents also reported that shoes are made up of plastic, chappal is made up of rubber while leather is used for making *Mojadia.*

Changing Trend in Footwear

The Table 4.42 reveals that 6 decades back majority of Bhil males wear *mojadi* as reported by respondents of the old age group, while younger group reported that two decade back both chappal and *mojadi* are worn by Bhil males.

From Table 4.41 and Table 4.42 it can be concluded that 6 decades back the Bhil males wear mojadi. But with the passage of time chappal is slowly adopted by these people and today few are shifted towards shoes also.

Accessories

The accessories which are used along with costume are bow

and arrow, axe, and few young males tie coloured synthetic scarf around the neck.

Table 4.42 : Trend of Bhil males Wearing different Footwears fro last 6 Decades

Age Group	Young N=20		Middle N=20		Old N=20	
	Last 2 decades		Last 4 decades		Last 6 decades	
	No.	%	No.	%	No.	%
Bare foot	–	–	3	15	5	35
Chappal	9	45	4	20	-	-
Mojadi	11	55	13	65	15	75

Between 2-6 decades also bows and arrows are the integral part of Bhil male costume. Some of them also kept lathi and axe with them. Thus it is generalized that no major change is observed in the Bhil male accessories.

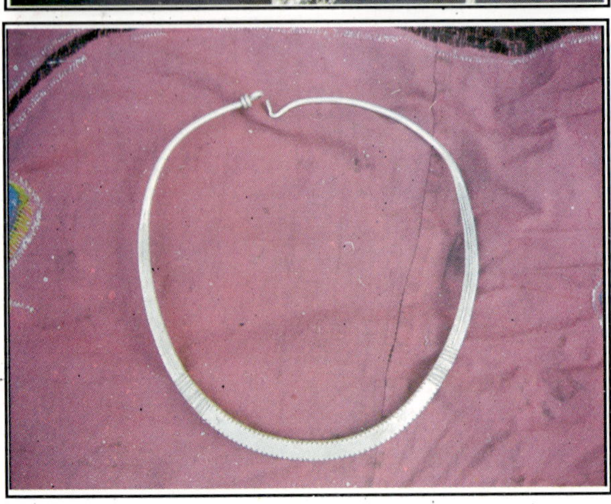

JEWELLERY OF GARASIA TRIBE

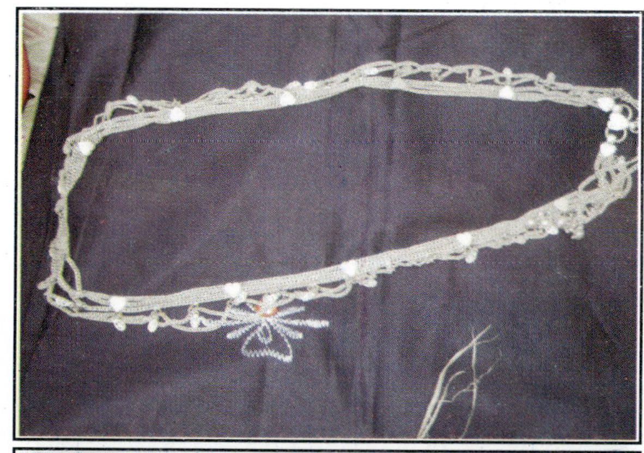

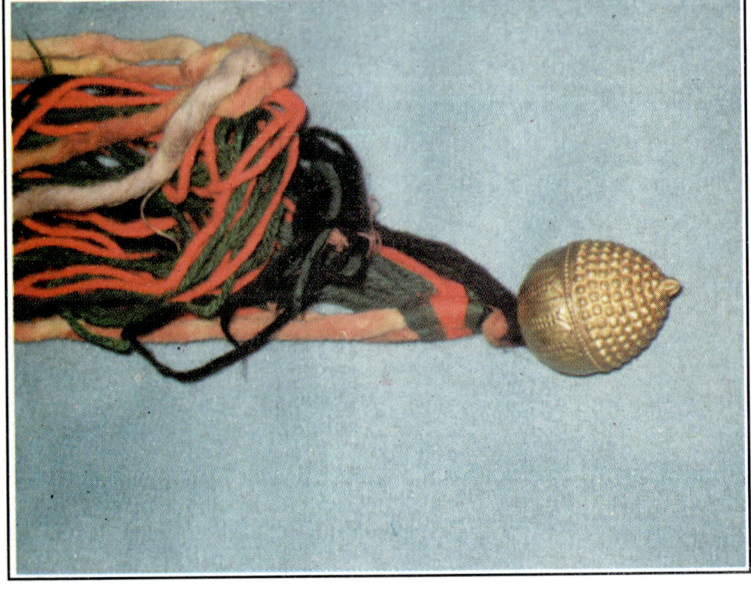

CHANGING TRENDS IN GARASIA COSTUME

GHAGHRA — THE TRADITIONAL LOWER GARMENT

BLACK BEAD HAAR

GARASIA WOMAN WITH
TRDITIONAL DRESS AND ORNAMENTS

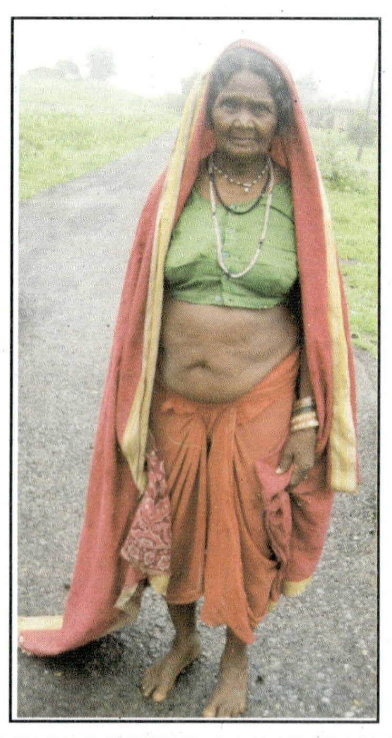

TRADITIONAL COSTUME OF KATHODI TRIBE

CHANGING COSTUME OF KATHODI TRIBE

JEWELLERY OF KATHODI TRIBE

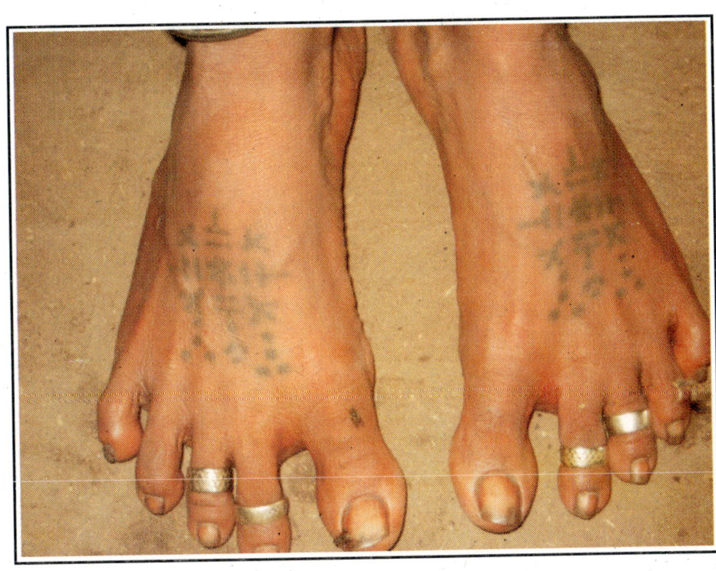

CHANGING TRENDS IN BHIL COSTUME

JEWELLERY OF BHIL TRIBE

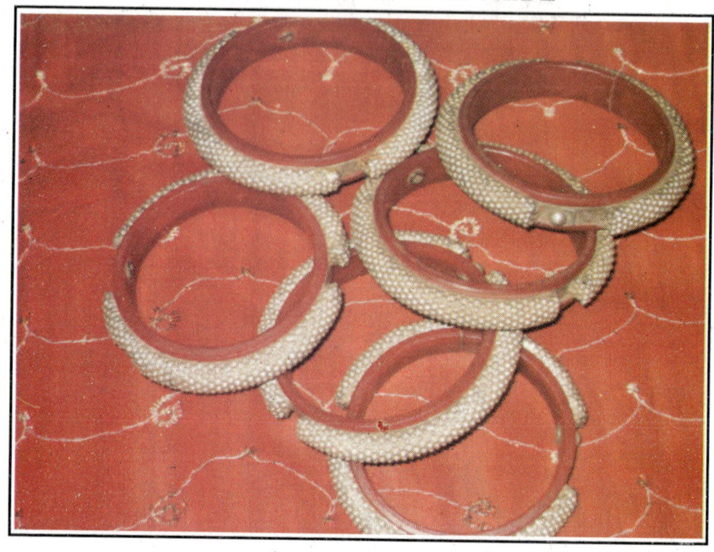

JULKI — THE TRADITIONAL UPPER GARMENT

TRADITIONAL COSTUME OF BHIL WOMAN

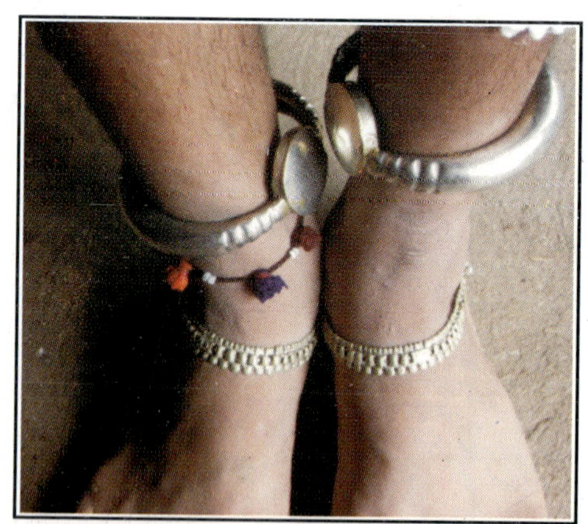

TRADITIONAL COSTUME OF DAMORE TRIBE

CHANGING TRENDS IN DAMORE COSTUME

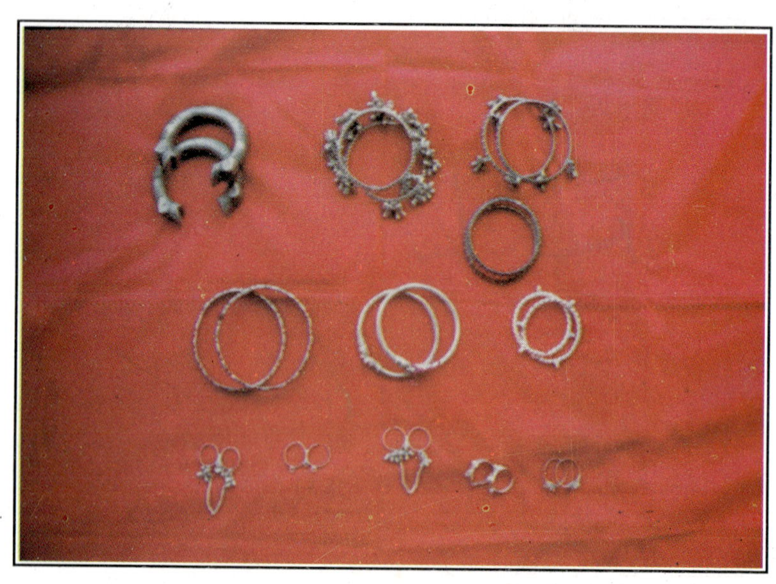

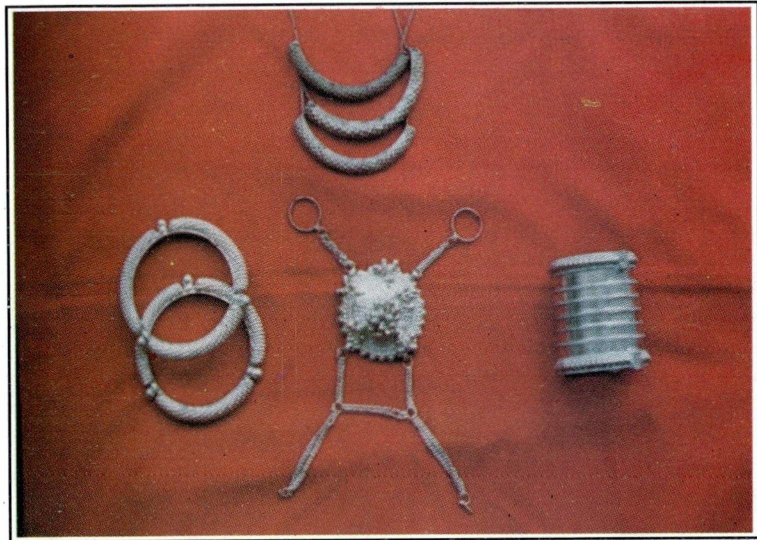

JEWELLERY OF DAMORE TRIBE

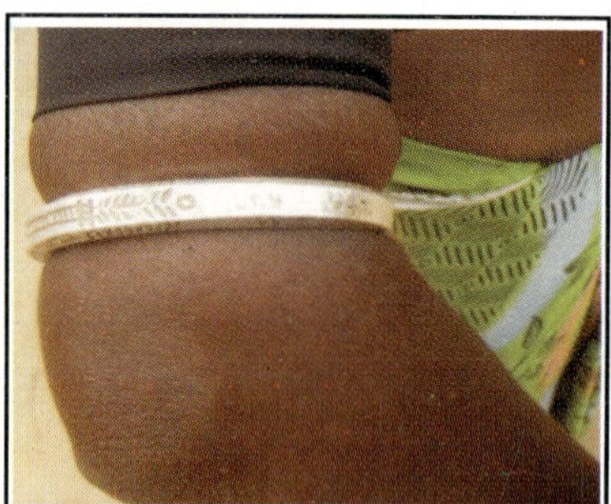

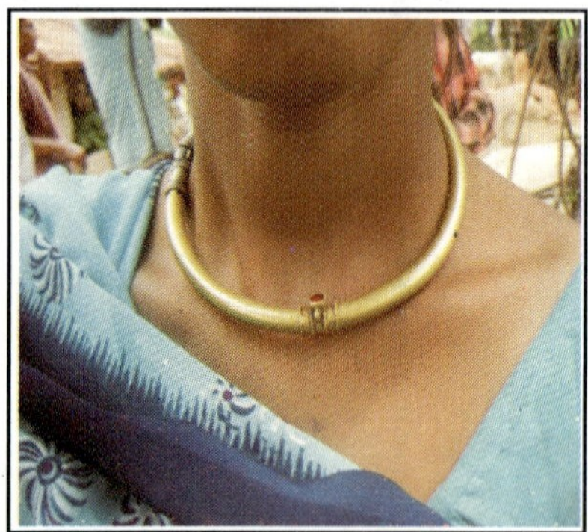

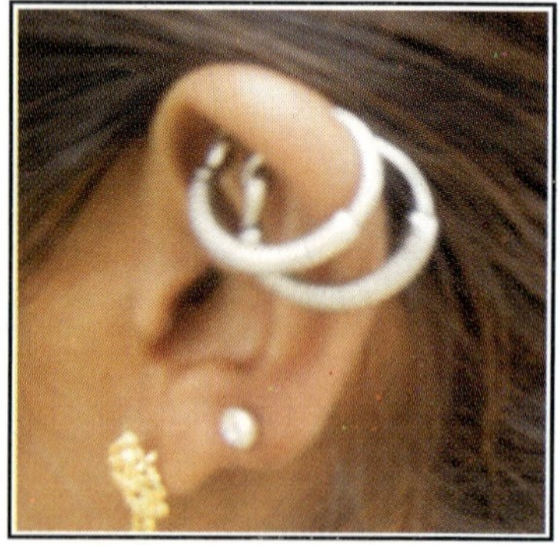

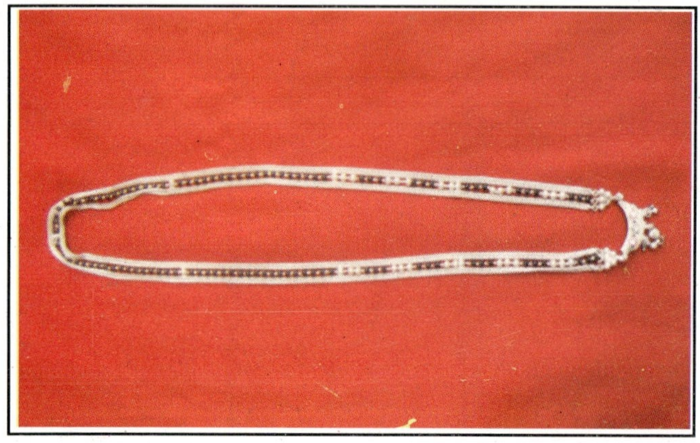

of the stripes are decorated with the contrast colour fabric, embroidery, and some multicolour triangle.

Fitting style of the Female Upper Garments

The Garasias females are very particular about the fitting of their upper garment. They prefer only proper fitted upper garment.

Use of Ready made, Tailormade and Homemade Upper Garments

Table 5.2 reveals that none of the respondent wear homemade upper garment, and 71 per cent prefer Tailormade, while only 28 per cent go for readymade ones. The switching of *Jhulki* is very difficult therefore these people are unable the prepare at home. Now a days it is also available in the local market with good embellishment, so young girls go for readymade *Jhulki*. But maximum females still prefer only tailormade *Jhulki* because of their rigidity towards fittings.

Table 5.2: Distribution of Garasia Female Respondents for the Use of Ready made, Tailormadeb and Homemade Upper Garments at Present

Particulars	Young N=20		Middle N=20		Old N=20		Total N=60	
	No.	%	No.	%	No.	%	No.	%
Readymade	10	50	7	35	–	–	17	28.33
Tailormade	10	50	13	65	20	100	43	71.66
Homemade	–	–	–	–	–	–	–	–

Changing Tend in use of Readymade Tailormadeand and Homemade Upper Garments

A decade prior from present only tailormade *Jhulki* was prevalent. As this upper garment is not available in the market and due to its difficult stitching women are unable to prepare it at home.

Fabric Details

(i) Type of Fabric Available and Preferred for Upper Garment

Cotton and synthetic both type of fabric are readily available in the market.

Table 5.3: Distribution of Garasia Female Respondents Regarding Fabric Preference for Upper Garment used at Present

Particulars	Young N=20		Middle N=20		Old N=20		Total N=60	
	No.	%	No.	%	No.	%	No.	%
Cotton	–	–	–	–	4	20	4	6.6
Synthetic	20	100	20	100	16	80	56	93.44

Findings of Table-5.3 highlight the fact that today synthetic topic is the mainly preferred i.e. 93 per cent women go for synthetic and only 6 per cent prefer cotton. The cotton is only preferred by old women the young & middle go for synthetic.

The reasons reported by the respondents for preference for synthetic:

(1) Bright colours

(2) No colour bleeding

(3) Easy to care

(4) No colour fading

(5) Durability

(ii) Colour choice in Upper Garments

They wear all bright colours such as yellow, orange, green, blue, red, etc. They does not have any restriction of colour. These women are fond of wearing bright colour. This tribe is specially known for its colourful dressing.

(iii) Fabric Prints of Upper Garments

The *Jhulki* is of plain fabric contrast colour bias strips are used on its outer edges in order to make it more attractive & beautiful.

Changing Trend in Fabric Details

Two decade prior mainly cotton fabric was used for *Jhulki.* The synthetic fabric was not easily available and the cost of synthetic was comparatively high than that of cotton. No other change was reported by the respondents.

Decoration of Upper Garment

The decoration plays an important role in the Garasia upper garment. Multicolour fabric triangles are attached at the armhole and neckline. Golden lace (Kinari) is also stitched at the neckline and in front of the *Jhulki.* Embroidery motifs are also prepared in the front and at the pannel of the *Jhulki.*

The strings are also decorated with golden lace and other accessories on different occasions they wear heavily decorated bright colour *Jhulki.* They use to embroider their name and their friends name on the *Jhulki.*

II. LOWER GARMENT

The female lower garment is *Ghaghra.* All the Garasia women regardless of their age they use to wear 8-20 meter width *Ghaghra,* with maggi at the botton. This maggi is of contrast bright colour and always cut bias.

(ii) Fabric Requirement

(*a*) ***Gherdar Ghaghra:*** 8-20 m. fabric is used in this type of *ghaghra.* Contrast colour fabric is used for *Magji* at the hemline this may be silver block printed or embroidered. The *ghaghra* is generally multi colour.

(*b*) **Pleated *Ghaghra:*** This is prepared in 2% to 3 m. fabric, with deep fold at the hemline. Side pleats are made in this *ghaghra.*

Use of Readymade, Tailormade and Homemade Lower Garment

Table 5.4 highlight the fact that none of the respondent prefer homemade lower garment and preference for readymade and Tailormade garment is approximately 50-50.

Table 5.4: Distribution of Garasia Female Respondents for the use of Reach Made, Tailormade & Homemade Lower Garment used at Present

Particulars	Young N=20		Middle N=20		Old N=20		Total N=60	
	No.	%	No.	%	No.	%	No.	%
Readymade	12	60	12	60	7	35	31	51.66
Tailormade	8	40	8	40	13	65	29	48.33
Homemade	–	–	–	–	–	–	–	–

The Garasia females does not know the basics of stitching therefore they prefer either homemade or tailomade garments

Table 5.5: Distribution of Garasia Female Respondents using different Lower Garments at Present

Particulars	Young N=20		Middle N=20		Old N=20		Total N=60	
	No.	%	No.	%	No.	%	No.	%
Gherdar Ghaghra	10	50	15	75	20	100	45	75
Pleated Ghaghra	10	50	5	25	-	-	15	25

Table 5.5 reveals that around 75 per cent Garasia women wear *Gherdar Ghaghra* which is their traditional lower garment, and only 25 per cent go for pleated *ghaghra.*

This table clearly shows that Garasia women are still adhere to their traditional costume.

Changing Trend in Female Lower Garment

It is reported by the females that prior to two decades only traditional *Ghaghra* was prevalent and worn by these females.

Design details of lower Garment

(i) Length

(*a*) *Gherdar Ghaghra*–Its length is 2″ above the ankle.

(*b*) Pleated *Ghaghra*–Its length is full i.e. upto ankle.

(ii) Fabric Print of Lower Garment

Table 5.6: Distribution of Garasia Female Respondents for Fabric Print of Lower Garments used at Present

Fabric Print	Young N=20		Middle N=20		Old N=20		Total N=60	
	No.	%	No.	%	No.	%	No.	%
Plain	4	20	12	60	10	50	26	43.33
Printed	16	80	8	40	10	50	34	56.6

The Table 5.6 reveals the fact that young females prefer more printed lower garment than plain ones. But on the whole 56 per cent females prefer printed and 43 per cent go for plain lower garment. Thus both plain and printed lower garments are worn by these females. The print is usually floral print.

Changing Trend in Fabric Details

It is reported by the females that most of the females prefer cotton plain *ghaghra* as their lower garment.

Decoration used for Lower Garment

Garasia females do not prefer plain *ghaghra*. *Ghaghra* is generally decorated with embroidery, silver block print at the *magji*, mirror, *sitara* work and they prefer only readymade & trailormade garments.

Changing Trend in use of Readymade, Tailormade and Homemade Lower Garments

Prior to two decades only tailormade lower garments were prevalent. The availability of readymade lower garment is started from 2 decade only. With the availability the preference for readymade garment started.

Fabric Details

(i) Type of Fabric available and Preferred for Lower Garment

The cotton and synthetic both are readily available in the market. For *Gherdar Ghaghra* only cotton fabric is used, it may be plain or printed and for pleated *Ghaghra* only synthetic fabric is used.

(ii) Colour Preference

In response to the colour preference in lower garment it is found that these females wear all bright colours such as Red, Green, Blue, Orange, Yellow and flourscent colours. The females are very much fond of decorated dresses. Their casual dress is also either embroidered or block printed.

III. COIFFURE

Headdress

During the field visit it was found that *Odhni* is the only headdress worn by Garasia females. The *Odhni* is made up of 4 m. fabric. 2 m. fabric is stitched width wise to the another 2 m. fabric, thus a square *Odhni* is being prepared.

Style of Wearing *Odhni*

The centre of the *Odhni* is draped on the head and both the ends fall on the sides of the hand. The bossom remain uncovered by the *Odhni.*

Changing Trend in Headdress

No change is reported by the females from last 6 decade the Garasia women are wearing only one type *Odhni* which is prevalent today.

Fabric Details

Cotton is the only fabric used for *Odhni.* It is either plain or printed. The floral print is most preferred for *Odhni.* Regarding the colour, all the bright flourscent colours such as orange, green yellow, purple, blue, etc. are used.

They generally prefer golden lace on all the four sides of the *Odhni..* Plain *Odhni* is also decorated with lace. No change is reported regarding the fabric details of *Odhni* since last 6 decades.

Hair Style

They use to braid their hair. These women are fond of decorating their hair, i.e. through Bright colours pins, ribbon, peals, etc.

As due to improved transportation facility the various cosmetic items popular in urban areas have reached to these remote areas also. Therefore the preference changes as change came in fashion.

IV. ORNAMENTS

Jewellery

Garasia females are very fond of jewellery they use to wore number of designer jewellery made up of different materials. Their maximum jewellery is made through silver and some are of gold and small beads.

Table 5.7: Jewellery worn by Garasia Women on different Body Parts

Sl.No.	Body Part	Name of Jewellery	Weight of Jewellery
1	2	3	4
1.	Head	Jhela	80-150 gm
		Bor	10-20 gm

1	2	3	4
2.	Nose	Long	5-10 gm (Gold)
3.	Ear	Ognia	50-60 gm
		Toti	50-60 gm
		Barli	20-30 gm
4.	Neck	Horki (small)	60-70 gm
		Horki (Big)	200-250 gm
		Hash	Small beads
		Haar	Small white & Mahroom beads
5.	Hand	Chudi	50-100 gm (with plastic chudi inside)
		Boliyo	Plastic Bangles
		Gajara	100-300 gm
		Todiyan	60-80 gm
6.	Finger	Viti	5 -20 gm
		Hathful	80-150 gm
7.	Waist	Kandora	60-250 gm
8.	Ankle	Kadora	500-800 gm
		Jajab	150-250 gm
9.	Toe	Bichhia	5-35 gm

The weight of every ornament vary according to individual preference. The females prefer heavy jewellery. Generally silver is used, the special jewellery of this tribe is *Haar* of small beads, this *Haar* is prepared by the women itself and it is very decorative and farcy. It is three type, one is tightly fitted to the neck which is of black beads with some yellow and red decoration, secondly fitted white bead *haar* with hangings at the end and thirdly long *Haar* of white beads with different colour beads for design. These are generally prepared before *mela* so that they wear these *Haar* during the *mela* and enjoy.

Tattooing

Every Garasia women use to tattoo his hand. These women generally tattoo their name on their hands. Various designs are also made through tatooing such as sun, flower, moon, etc. It is generally done in the *mela.*

This is generally done at the age of 8-10 years.

Improving appearance: These females are very fond of make-up. They use cream, powder, *Bindi, Kajal,* Lipstick, Nailpoint, etc. They are always eger to opt the new cosmetic material which improve their beauty. The use of this material is increasing day-by-day.

V. FOOTWEAR

These females wear chappal as their footwear. Generally Rubber sleeper are common among these people.

Changing Trend in Footwear

The Table 5.8 reveals that about 90 per cent Garasia females remain bare foot 6 decades before. As the time passes, their preference towards chappal increases. As 2 decade prior only 10 per cent female remain bare foot, while 90 per cent wear chappal.

Table 5.8: Trend of Garasia Female Wwearing different Footwears in last 6 Decades

Footwear	Young N=20		Middle N=20		Old N=20	
	Last 2 decades		Last 4 decades		Last 6 decades	
	No.	%	No.	%	No.	%
Bare foot	2	10	14	70	18	90
Chappal	18	90	6	30	2	10

Thus it can be concluded that with the passage of time the preference for chappal increases.

II. GARASIA MALE COSTUME

Upper

The two types of upper garments are famous among this tribe i.e. *Kurta* and Shirt. During investigation it is found that the male garments are much of more influenced with the modernisation. As men are going out for work and came in contact with urban area. This exposure ultimately result and is easily seen in their costume i.e. now most of the Garasia men are wearing pant and shirt as their costume instead of *Dhoti* and *Kurta.*

Their traditional costume was *Bandi* and *Dhoti* which is later taken over by *Kurta* and *Dhoti* and presently these are taken over by pant and Shirt.

The over thing which does change is the use of towel or *Pheta* along with their costume. This *Pheta* is of red colour or of any light, colour towel. This *Pheta* is being tied on their head or kept around the neck for use. The fabric details design detail colour preference and fabric print are same as that of Bhil male costume.

6 Costumes of Damors and Changing Trend

In the view of the study the findings regarding Damor costumes have been discussed in detail in this chapter.

FEMALE COSTUME

I. UPPER GARMENT

The upper garment worn by the Damor female is blouse. Every respondent whether she is young or old wore only blouse.

No change was reported by the respondents regarding the upper garment. Since independence they wore blouse as their upper garment, only the length may vary according to individual preference.

Design Details of Upper Garment

(i) Neckline: The most common shape in the neckline is round, some young females prefer square, glass or pentagonal also.

(ii) *Opening:* The opening is generally in the centre front. They use hook and eye as well as button and button hole as fastners.

(iii) *Sleeve:* The set in sleeve is used in the blouse. It is snugly fitted on the arms and its length is 7″ to 8″ i.e. above the elbow.

(iv) *Length:* The blouse length vary from 2″ to 6″ above the waist line.

Fitting Style of Upper Garment

The young Damor females used to wear fitted blouse while, middle and old ones generally wear semifitted blouse.

Use of Readymade, Tailormade and Homemade Upper Garment

All the respondents reported that they use only tailormade upper garment mainly in order to get the proper fitting of the blouse.

The body structure of every individual is different and the good fitting is required for the blouse therefore Damor female prefer tailormade blouse so that their need will be satisfied.

Changing trend in use of Readymade, Tailormade and Homemade upper Garments

Table 6.1 Clearly reveals that maximum Damor females prefer Tailormade upper garment. 6 decade back only 40 per cent women do stitching at home and no one prefer readymade garment.

Fabric Details

(i) ***Type of fabric available and preferred for upper garment:*** Cotton and synthetic both the fabrics are readily available in the local market. The old female prefer only cotton fabric while, middle and young ones generally go for synthetic mainly due to the lusture and durability.

Table 6.1: Trend in use of Readymade, Tailormade and Homemade Upper Garments of Women from last 6 Decades

Particulars	Young N=20		Middle N=20		Old N=20	
	Last 2 decades		Last 4 decades		Last 6 decades	
	No.	%	No.	%	No.	%
Readymade	–	–	–	–	–	–
Tailormade	20	100	15	75	12	60
Homemade	–	–	5	25	8	40

(ii) *Colour choice in upper garment:* In response to the colour preference in the upper garment it is found that young Damor, female's favourite colour is black because it matches with every colour. Other than black they prefer yellow, blue, red, green and all other bright colours.

(iii) *Fabric prints of upper garments:* Upper garment worn by Damor female is plain. They does not prefer any print on their blouse.

No change was reported by the respondents regarding the colour, print, fabric choice of upper garment.

II. LOWER GARMENT

The lower garment is basically of two styles i.e. pleated *ghaghra* and petticoat.

Table 6.2: Distribution of Damor Females Preference Regarding Lower Garment at Present

Particulars	Young N=20		Middle N=20		Old N=20		Total N=60	
	No.	%	No.	%	No.	%	No.	%
Pleated Ghaghra	–	–	5	25	20	100	25	41.66
Petticoat	20	100	15	75	–	–	35	58.33

Table-6.2 reveals that young Damor females wear only petticoat, *ghaghra* while, old female wear only pleated one the middleagers prefer both the types.

The preference towards pleated *ghaghra* increases with the increase in age. This is because the gher in the pleated one is more than that of petticoat one therefore pleated *ghaghra* is more comfortable while, working than petticoat *ghaghra*.

Changing Trend in Lower garment: No change was reported by these respondents. The similar preference for pleated *ghaghra* & petticoat remain according to the age.

6 decade back the embroidery was not prevalent in the petticoat only long frill was attached to the lower side to provide ease while, walking.

Design Details of Lower Garment

(i) Length

(a) ***Pleated ghaghra:*** The length of this *ghaghra* is full i.e. upto ankle

(b) ***Petticoat ghaghra:*** The length of this *ghaghra* is full i.e. upto ankle.

(ii) Fabric Requirement

(a) ***Pleated ghaghra:*** The fabric requirement for this type *of ghaghra* is $3^1/_2$ meter. (knife pleats are made and therefore the fabric requirement is directly proportional to the width of pleat and waist size).

(b) ***Petticoat:*** Two to two and a half meter fabric is required for petticoat. In this type at the bottom a wide embroidered panel is attached and therefore if requires plain fabric.

Fabric Details

(i) Type of fabric available and preferred for lower garment

At present both cotton and synthetic are readily available in the market.

Table 6.3: Distribution of Damor Female Respondents for Present Fabric Preference for Lower Garment

Fabric	Young N=20		Middle N=20		Old N=20		Total N=60	
	No.	%	No.	%	No.	%	No.	%
Cotton	–	–	5	25	10	50	15	25
Synthetic	20	100	15	75	10	50	45	75

Table 6.3 reveals that 25 per cent females prefer cotton while, 75 per cent go for synthetic fabric. Young females does not prefer cotton while, preference for cotton is more among old age group.

(ii) Colour preferences

They wear all types of colours bright as well as dull i.e. red, yellow, orange, black, brown, grey, etc.

Fabric Print of Lower Garment

The petticoat is worn of plain fabric while, pleated *ghaghra* is printed one. The common prints in the *ghaghra* are floral prints.

III. COIFFURE

1. Headdress

During the field visit it was observed that *Odhni* was the headdress worn by the Damor females by all the three age groups. The length of the *Odhni* is $1^1/_2$ m. and width is 1m. only. Some of the females have also started wearing *saree* which stays one right shoulder.

Style of Wearing *Odhni*

The centre of the *Odhni* is tucked at the head and both the ends are left open or sometimes tucked into the *ghaghra*. The bassom are not covered by the *Odhni* they remain bare.

No change was reported by these females. Between 2-6 decade the similar *Odhni* was prevalent. They used to wore only plain *Odhni*. At present printed and double colour *Odhni* are also prevalent.

Fabric Details

(i) Type of Fabric Available and Preferred

Both cotton and synthetic an readily available in the local market.

Table 6.4: Distribution of *Damor* female respondents for fabric preference for headdress use at present

Fabric	Young N=20		Middle N=20		Old N=20		Total N=60	
	No.	%	No.	%	No.	%	No.	%
Cotton	2	10	9	45	12	60	23	38.33
Synthetic	18	90	11	55	8	40	37	61.66

Table-6.4 highlight the fact that around 61 per cent women prefer synthetic *Odhni* and 38 per cent go for cotton. The younger females wear more synthetic *Odhni* than cotton ones.

(ii) Colours Preferred

The Damor females wear all types colours viz. red, yellow, green, purple, black, grey, etc.

(iii) Fabric Prints

Plain and printed both are preferred by the females. Floral print is most common among Damors.

Changing Trend in Fabric Details

It was reported by the respondents that between 1 to 2 decade both the type of fabric were used in *Odhni* but prior to that only cotton *Odhni* was used.

No colour restriction was reported and prints were also common as present.

2. Hair style

Two types of hair style are common among Damor females i.e. open and braided style. This observation is same as in the Bhil tribe.

Females love to apply some fancy pins, buckole, ribbons in their hair. Oiling of hair is compulsory task in this tribe. Sometimes they also cut their hair and make them short for open.

Changing trend in Hair style

Hair style was same only the decoration is increased between 4-6 decade the women does not do any decoration and with the passage of time it increases.

IV. ORNAMENTS

Jewellery

Damor females were also fond of jewellery and wore different types of jewellery on different body parts.

Table 6.5: Jewellery Worn by Damor Women on Different Body Parts

Sl. No.	Body Part	Name of jewellery	Weight of jewellery
1	2	3	4
1.	Head	Bor	10-15 gm
2.	Nose	Long	3-8 gm
3.	Ear	Caap	8-10 gm
		Bali	10-15 gm
		Tops	8-15 gm
4.	Neck	Chain	50-70 gm
		Ahadi	150-250 gm
		Hasli	10 gm Gold &

1	2	3	4
		Mangalsutra	100-150 gm silver 30-60 gm
5.	Hand	Bangdi Kada	30-50 gm 20-30 gm
6.	Finger	Vatla	5-15 gm
7.	Ankal	Toda	50-200 gm
8.	Toe	Machali	30-60 gm

The weight of the jewellery vary according to the individual choice. The maximum jewellery is made up of silver only few such as long and *Hash* may have gold in them.

Changing Trend in Jewelllery

The major change reported by the respondents that these ornaments were heavier in earlier times than of the present era.

Tattooing

Every Damor female have tattooing on her hand and may have tattoos on head and feets along with the hand. They generally tattoo their name on their, hand with various designs viz. sun, star, bird, etc.

V. FOOTWEAR

These women are much concerned about their dressing concerned about their and looks therefore they wear different fancy chappals available in their local market. But in routine they wear simple sponge chappal. These women do great care of their footwear's.

Male Costume

The male costume of Damor tribe is exactly same that of Bhil tribe i.e. *Kurta, Dhoti,* and turban. As reported by the respondents that the young generation have start wearing pant and shirt instead of *Dhoti-Kurta.* All the observations and reporting by the Damor's is similar to that of Bhils in all areas regarding lower garment, upper garment, coiffure, jewellery, footwear and other accessories.

Costumes of Kathodis and Changing Trend

In the view of the study the findings regarding Kathodi costumes have been discussed in detail in this chapters.

FEMALE COSTUME

I. UPPER GARMENT

The prevalent upper garments among the Kathodi female are given in the Table 7.1.

Table 7.1: Trend in use of Kathodi Readymadc, Tailormade and Homemade Upper Garments of Damore Women from last 6 Decades

Particulars	Young N=20		Middle N=20		Old N=20		Total N=60	
	No.	%	No.	%	No.	%	No.	%
Kanchali	–	–	–	–	3	15	3	5
Blouse	20	100	20	100	17	85	57	95

Table 7.1 reveals a clear picture that both young & middle age group prefer only blouse and only 15 per cent old age people go for *kanchali* as their upper garment.

Thus it is clearly observed that 95 per cent women wore blouse and only 5 per cent women go for *kanchali.*

This shift was manly due to the unavailability of *kanchali* in the readymade market. The stiching of blouse is quite easier than that of *kanchali* therefore the tailor prefer to stitch blouse rather than *kanchali.*

Changing trend in Female Upper Garments

Looking to the Table 7.2 it was found that 6 decades prior only *kanchali* was worn by the females, but as the time passes the blouse came into picture 2 decades before only 25 per cent women wore *kanchali* while, 75 per cent sifted to the blouse.

Table 7.2: Trend of Kathodi Female Upper Garments in for last 6 Decades

Costume	Young N=20		Middle N=20		Old N=20	
	Last 2 decades		Last 4 decades		Last 6 decades	
	No.	%	No.	%	No.	%
Kanchali	5	25	18	90	20	100
Blouse	15	75	2	10	–	–

Fitting Style of the Female Upper Garments

Table 7.3: Distribution of Damore Female Respondents for Present Fabric Preference for Lower Garment

Fitting style	Young N=20		Middle N=20		Old N=20		Total N=60	
	No.	%	No.	%	No.	%	No.	%
Fitted	20	100	18	90	8	40	46	76.66
Semi fitted	–	–	2	10	12	60	14	23.33
Loose	–	–	–	–	–	–	–	–

Table 7.3 gives a clear picture that more than 75 per cent women prefer fitted upper garment and semifitted was preferred by 23 per cent and no *Kathodi* women go for loose fitting garment.

It was also reported by the respondents that were very particular about the fitting of the garment.

Use of Tailormade & Homemade Upper Garments

Table 7.4 reveals that young and middle age group women prefer only tailormade garments. It was the only old group from which 25 per cent women adopt-tailormade also.

Table 7.4: Distribution of Kathodi Female Respondents for Fabric Preference for Reads Made, Tailormade and Homemade upper Garments at Present

Fitting style	Young N=20		Middle N=20		Old N=20		Total N=60	
	No.	%	No.	%	No.	%	No.	%
Readymade	-	-	-	-	5	25	5	8.33
Tailormade	20	100	20	100	15	75	55	91.66
Homemade	-	-	-	-	-	-	-	-

It was reported during the communication that these women does not have any knowledge about stitching. They are even handicap in repairing the torned garment. Changing trend in use of Readymade, Tailormade and Homemade upper garments.

Table 7.5: Trend in use of Readymade, tailor made and Home made upper garments of Kathodi female from last 6 decades

Costume	Young N=20		Middle N=20		Old N=20	
	Last 2 decades		Last 4 decades		Last 6 decades	
	No.	%	No.	%	No.	%
Readymade	8	40	–	–	–	–
Tailormade	12	60	20	100	20	100
Homemade	–	–	–	–	–	–

Table 7.5 reveals that 6 decade back women use only tailormade upper garment. Thus it can be concluded that in the early ages also women do not know the art of stitching work. As the time passes the preference for readymade garment increases and gradually about 40 per cent women shifted to readymade upto last 2 decades.

Fabric Details

(i) Type of Fabric available and preferred for Upper Garment

Cotton and Polyester were the two readily available fabric in the Kathodi market. During the field visit it was observed that cotton is most liked fabric but due to its high cost it is quite difficult for them to purchase. Therefore they are started wearing polyester fabric through number of colours and prints available in it. Maximum women started wearing synthetic plain fabric for their upper garment. As reported by the respondents the synthetic is easy to maintain and wash.

(ii) Colours choice in Upper Garment

Regarding colour choice these people are not much concerned, they wore which ever it available easily. In their community there is no boundation of colours. Young women generally wear bright and printed upper garment, while, other have no such specific choice.

(iii) Fabric Prints of Upper Garments

The Table 7.6 reveals that all the three age group used to wear plain fabric over printed fabric for their upper garment as indicated by their per centage i.e. 60 per cent females of young age group 75 per cent females of middle age group and 100 per cent of old age group. However printed fabrics are most prevalent among young females where 40 per cent of the respondents are using printed fabric in their upper garment. On an average, it can be observed that more than

73 per cent respondents wear plain while, printed upper garment are worn only by 26 per cent.

Table 7.6: Distribution of Kathodi Female Respondents for Fabric Prints in Upper Garments used at Present

Particulars	Young N=20		Middle N=20		Old N=20		Total N=60	
	No.	%	No.	%	No.	%	No.	%
Plain	12	60	15	75	20	100	44	73.33
Printed	8	40	5	25	–	–	16	26.66

The main reason of wearing plain fabric upper garment is that it costs lower and matches or make contrast with different printed lower garment. Small floral prints most commonly used in blouse.

Changing Trend in Fabric Details

(i) Type of fabric available and preferred for upper garments

Findings of the Table 7.7 highlight the fact that synthetic fabric is available in the local market from last 2 decades only as reported by the respondents. Earlier to that only cotton are used. But with the emergence of synthetic fabric the preference for synthetic fabric increased and today maximum females are using synthetic fabric as their upper garments.

Table 7.7: Trend of Fabric available and Preferred for Upper Garments by Kathodi Female

Fabric	Young N=20		Middle N=20		Old N=20	
	Last 2 decades		Last 4 decades		Last 6 decades	
	No.	%	No.	%	No.	%
Cotton	8	40	20	100	20	100
Synthetic	12	60	–	–	–	–

(ii) Colour Choice in Upper Garment

From the earlier time this tribal group had no restrictions of colour therefore they wear all the colours which are readily available in the market. But at the time of marriage the bride wore red colour upper garment as its full dress is of read colour.

(iii) Fabric Prints of Upper Garment

No change was reported by the respondents in the fabric prints of upper garment. Every age group said that from early ages mainly plain was womed by every women and some times for the change and due to personal interest the women started wearing printed.

Decoration of Upper Garment

In their routine days they does not do any decoration. But on occasions and festival time they wear worked or embroidered upper garment. This trend was followed from last 6 decades as reported by the respondents of all the age groups.

II. LOWER GARMENT

The female lower garment is basically of two styles. They were pleated *ghaghra* and *petticoat ghaghra.*

Table 7.8: Distribution of Kathodi Female Respondents using different lower Garments at Present

Particulars	Young N=20		Middle N=20		Old N=20		Total N=60	
	No.	%	No.	%	No.	%	No.	%
Pleated Ghaghra	2	10	10	50	5	25	17	28.33
Petticoat	18	90	10	50	–	–	28	46.66

Table 7.8 reveals out the fact that on the whole about 47 per cent Kathodi females wore *petticoat* followed by pleated *ghaghra* (28%). It is reported by the old Kathodi females that

they wear only *saree* in the form *of Dhoti* as their lower garment therefore due to its style of wearing they does not require any lower garment. That firstly the adoption of lower garment and later the change in its style was the direct indication of impact of urban areas on the tribal people. The *petticoat* worn by young Bhil females seems to be an adoption of *petticoat* which is most common lower garment worn by urban females under *saree.* However old females still wore their traditional lower garment i.e. *dhoti saree.*

Changing Trend in Female Lower Garments

Table 7.9 reveal that between 4-6 decades only *Dhoti saree* is worn by Kathodi female as reported by middle and old age group females and pleated *ghaghra & petticoat* are used from last 2 decades by a few respondents of young age group.

Table 7.9: Trend of Kathodi Female lower Garments from last 6 Decades

Costume	Young N=20		Middle N=20		Old N=20	
	Last 2 decades		Last 4 decades		Last 6 decades	
	No.	%	No.	%	No.	%
Pleated Ghaghra	8	40	–	–	–	–
Petticoat Ghaghra	2	10	–	–	–	–
Dhoti saree	10	50	20	100	20	100

Design details of Lower Garment

(i) Length

(*a*) Pleated *Ghaghra*–The length of this *ghaghra* was full i.e. upto ankle.

(*b*) *Petticoat:* The length of this was full i.e. upto ankle.

(*c*) *Dhoti saree:* Its length vary according to individual choice i.e. may be upto knee, between knee & ankle and upto ankle.

(ii) Fabric Requirement

(*a*) Pleated *Ghaghra:* The fabric required for this type *of ghaghra* is 3 meter.

(*b*) *Petticoat:* Two meter fabric is required for *petticoat ghaghra.* This is prepared by joining various pieces of pannels.

(*c*) *Dhoti Saree:* In this 5 m fabric or *saree* is being used.

Changing Trend in Design details of Lower Garments

In *petticoat* and pleated *ghaghra* no change is reported, but in the *Dhoti saree* before 2 decades 9 metre *saree* was used. It is worn in such a manner it works as a lower garment like *dhoti* as well as it covers the bossom part of the female.

Use of Readymade, Tailormade and Homemade Lower Garment

Table 7.10 Highlighted the fact that none of the respondents preferred home made lower garment. Out of three age groups only old females prefer readymade lower garment while, young ones gave more preference to the tailormade lower garment.

Table 7.10: Distribution of Kathodi Female Respondents for the use of Readymade, Tailormade and Homemade Lower Garments used at Present

Particulars	Young N=20		Middle N=20		Old N=20		Total N=60	
	No.	%	No.	%	No.	%	No.	%
Readymade	8	40	16	80	20	100	44	73.33
Tailormade	12	60	4	20	–	–	16	26.66
Homemade	–	–	–	–	–	–	–	–

On the whole it can be sum that more than 70 per cent females wear readymade garment and only 26 per cent wear tailormade

Changing Trend in use of Readymade, Tailormade and Homemade lower Garments

The Table 7.11 clarifies that according to middle and old age group females i.e. between 2-6 decade only readymade lower garment was prevalent. As in prior time only *Dhoti saree* was popular which does not require any stitching therefore it is used as a readymade garment.

Table 7.11: Trend of Kathodi Female use of Readymade, Tailormade and Homemade Lower Garments from last 6 Decades

Costume	Young N=20		Middle N=20		Old N=20	
	Last 2 decades		Last 4 decades		Last 6 decades	
	No.	%	No.	%	No.	%
Readymade	12	60	20	100	20	100
Tailormade	8	40	–	–	–	–
Homemade	–	–	–	–	–	–

Fabric Details

(i) Type of Fabric Available & Preferred for Lower Garment

For lower garments also cotton and synthetic are the two fabrics that are largely available in the local market, But the preference for a particular fabric vary according to the age group as shown in Table-7.12.

The Table 7.12 reveals a clear picture that in all the age groups synthetic fabric is the mostly preferred for lower garment. Only 11 per cent respondents go for cotton. The reasons for choosing the synthetic fabric are high strength, wash & wear property, good dimensional stability and elegant appearance.

Table 7.12: Distribution of Kathodi Female Respondents for Present Fabric Preference for Lower Garments

Particulars	Young N=20		Middle N=20		Old N=20		Total N=60	
	No.	%	No.	%	No.	%	No.	%
Cotton	–	–	2	10	56	25	7	11.66
Synthetic	20	100	18	90	15	75	53	88.33

(ii) Colour Preferences

It is reported by the females that they wear any colour in their lower garment.

(iii) Fabric Print of Lower Garment

During the field visit it is observed that the Kathodi women stated that they used to wear both plain & printed lower garment. These women does not have any specific choices regarding plain & printed.

The main, fabric prints are floral in nature and some young women also prefer some geometrical designs.

Changing Trend in Fabric Details

For lower garment i.e. *dhoti saree & ghaghra* only cotton fabric was available between 2-6 decades. From last 2 decades the synthetic fabrics area also available therefore preference for synthetic fabric increases over cotton.

As far as prints are concerned, they does not have any specific preference. These women prefer the fabric which is cheapest, without any preference of print or plain.

No decoration is done on the *ghaghra* only machine embroidery is done at few places. The coloured embroidery threads are used for embroidery. The motifs are usually leaves flowers.

Ceremonial Lower Garment

The *ghaghra* with some shining *sitara* work or golden, silver thread embroidered are worn by the women. The bride generally wear red *ghaghra* with golden work.

III. COIFFURE

1. Headdress

During field visit it is observed that *odhni* is the only headdress worn by the Kathodi women by all the three age groups. Those women who wear *dhoti saree* they use their *saree* itself as a headdress. The length and width of the *Odhni* is $1^1/_2$ by 1 m. It is worn by just tucked on to the head and both the ends were left open or sometimes tucked into the *ghaghra.*

Changing trend in Headdress

It is evident during data collection that between 2-6 decades no separate headdress is used only the *saree* wored as a headdress. Between last 2 decades the *Odhni* came into picture which is same as present *odhni.*

Fabric Details

(i) Type of Fabric available and Preferred

Both cotton and synthetic fabrics are largely available in the local market till 2 decades and the preference is also found for both the fabrics. But before 2 decades to 6 decades the cotton fabric is readily available and preferenced.

(ii) Colours Preferred

Kathodi female wear all the bright and dull colours without any discribancy.

(iii) Fabric print of Headdress

The headdress is usually plain only 'on certain occasions they wear printed *odhni* 2 decades before. Between 2-6 decade they wear *dhoti saree* as their headdress and lower garment which may or may not be prints.

2. Hair Style

The three types of hairstyles are prevalent among females i.e. open hair style, pony and braided style.

Table 7.13: Distribution of Kathodi Female Respondents for different Hairstyle used at Present

Particulars	Young N=20		Middle N=20		Old N=20		Total N=60	
	No.	%	No.	%	No.	%	No.	%
Open	6	30	–	–	–	–	6	10
Pony	12	60	6	30	–	–	18	30
Braided	2	10	14	70	20	100	36	6.0

Table 7.13 reveals that all the old women use to make braiding of their hair, while, in middle age group only 70 per cent women go for braiding and remaining prefer pony as their hair style. The young women are more concerned about their looks therefore they use all the three type is hairstyle according to the purpose or occasion.

Overall it is concluded free from this table that 60 per cent Kathodi women prefer braiding 30 per cent prepare pony and only 10 per cent kept their hair open. The braiding is done when they works in field and jungle where lot of din and dust flows and make their hair rough and entangled in one another. No special care is done of the hair. Only regular oiling is done and combed with very fine comb (Kasnghi).

Changing trend in Hairstyle

No difference is observed and reported in the Kathodi hairstyle from today to last 6 decades.

Hair Decoration

When Kathodi women went out from their home or in any

marriage they use to put some fancy hairpins, rubbers in their braid and young ones put hair bands, etc.

IV. ORNAMENTS

(1) Jewellery

Kathodi females are very fond of jewellery and wear different types of jewellery in different body parts i.e. neck, ear, head, ankle, toes, etc.

The weight of every ornament vary according to individual preference. Only Silver metal is used for different ornaments. Some of Kathodi women even use white metal for their ornament as they are unable to purchase silver ornaments.

Table 7.14: Jewellry worn by Kathodi Women on different Body Parts

Sl. No.	Body Part	Name of Jewellery	Weight of Jewellery
1.	Head	Bor Tika	10-15 gm 5-10 gm
2.	Nose	Long	3-5 gm
3.	Ear	Tokari Tops	10-20 gm 6-12 gm
4.	Neck	Chain Munglasutra Modlia	20-30 gm 30-50 gm 30-50 gm
5.	Hand	Kada Chudi	100-300 gm 10-15 gm
6.	Finger	Viti	5-15 gm
7.	Ankle	Pajab	50-100 gm
8.	Toe	Bichhia	5-15 gm

Changing Trend in Jewellery

Their is no change in the type of jewellery the only difference is reported in the weight of the ornaments. Previously the ornaments are of heavy weight as compared to today's ornaments.

(2) Tattooing

Tattooing is a type of body decoration done on different body parts. These are the permanent marks.

Table 7.15: Distribution of Kathodi female Respondents for Preference of Tattooing at Present

Particulars	Young N=20		Middle N=20		Old N=20		Total N=60	
	No.	%	No.	%	No.	%	No.	%
Preferred	18	90	20	100	20	100	58	96.66
Not preferred	2	10	–	–	–	–	23	3.33

The Table-7.15 shows the fact that Kathodi females preferred tattooing as indicated by the overall percentage i.e. 96.66 per cent. Only few of the young females i.e. 10 per cent reject the tattooing.

Thus it can be summarized that tattooing is considered commonly preferred body decoration. During interaction with Kathodi females they reported that their are number of body places where can be done these are-forehead, neck, arms, legs, cheeks & chin. In was generally done in green & blue colour. The common motifs are sun, moon, bird, peacock, name of the person, dots snack, flower, etc.

Changing Trend in Tattooing

From today to 6 decades back no change is reported by the respondents. As it is done mainly to improve the body appearance and every women wants to look beautiful therefore it is even increasing day by day.

V. FOOTWEAR

The Kathodi women reported that they wear chappal as their footwear. All the females regardless of their age they prefer only chappal, because it cheaper as well as easy to put on & take off.

Changing Tend in Footwear

Between 2-6 decade many women remain bare foot only when they move out for some functions or so they wear chappal. Prior to 2 decades maximum women started wearing chappal.

Male Costume

Upper Garment

Shirt is the only upper garment worn by the Kathodi males. All the males reported during interview that they wear only half sleeve shirt. As it is easy during work as well as easily available in the local market.

Changing trend in Upper Garment

Table 7.16 reveals that according to middle and old age respondents most of the male wear only *kurta* as their upper garment. During 4th decade shirt is also popular, while, earlier to that shirt is more preferred than *kurta*.

Table 7.16: Trend of Kathodi male upper Garment from Last 6 Decades

Costume	Young N=20		Middle N=20		Old N=20	
	Last 2 decades		Last 4 decades		Last 6 decades	
	No.	%	No.	%	No.	%
Kurta	7	35	16	80	20	100
Shirt	13	65	4	20	-	-

The design of the *kurta* and shirt is similar to that of Bhil shirt & *kurta*. No change is observed and reported by the Kathodi male.

Use of Readymade, Tailormade and Homemade upper garments

Table 7.17 gives a clear picture that none of the respondents use homemade upper garment and only 13 per cent prefer readymade ones. The maximum males go for Tailormade upper garment. Mainly due to proper fitting and secondly the variety are not available in readymade upper garment in the local market.

Table 7.17: Distribution of Kathodi Male Respondents for the use of Readymade, Tailormade and Homemade Upper Garments at Present

Particulars	Young N=20		Middle N=20		Old N=20		Total N=60	
	No.	%	No.	%	No.	%	No.	%
Readymade	6	30	2	10	–	–	8	13.33
Tailormade	14	70	18	90	20	100	52	86.66
Homemade	–	–	–	–	–	–	–	–

Changing trend in use of Readymade, Tailor made and Homemade Upper Garments

It is reported by all the age groups that before one decade only tailormade garments are preferred neither readymade nor homemade are available and preferred.

Hence it can be summarized that Kathodi tribe prefer Tailormade garments from last 6 decades.

Fabric Details

(i) Type of Fabric Available and Preferred for Upper Garment

Table 7.18 reveals the fact that today about 75 per cent males prefer synthetic fabric for upper garment while, remaining 25 per cent prefer cotton fabric. The young Kathodi male prefer only synthetic while, preference for both the fabric i.e. cotton & synthetic is observed in middle & old age group.

Table 7.18: Distribution of Kathodi Male Respondents for Present Fabric Preference for Upper Garments

Fabric	Young N=20		Middle N=20		Old N=20		Total N=60	
	No.	%	No.	%	No.	%	No.	%
Cotton	-	-	5	25	10	50	15	25
Synthetic	20	100	15	75	10	50	45	75

(ii) Colours preferred in the Upper Garment

In response to the colour preferences in the upper garment it is reported that in *Kurta* they prefer white, off-white, grey and Brown while, in shirts they wear any colour. On occasions they specially prefer bright colour shirts such as red, yellow, orange, blue etc.

(iii) Fabric print of Upper Garment

The *kurta* is generally of plain fabric and the shirt may or may not have prints. The common prints on upper garments are lines, checks, flowers, and other geometrical prints.

Changing Trends in Fabric Details

(i) Type of fabric available and preferred for upper garment

Table 7.19: Changing trend in Fabric Preference for Upper Garment by Kathodi Male

Costume	Young N=20		Middle N=20		Old N=20	
	Last 2 decades		Last 4 decades		Last 6 decades	
	No.	%	No.	%	No.	%
Cotton	13	65	20	100	20	100
Synthetic	7	35	-	-	-	-

Table 7.19 reveals that after 2 decade only cotton fabric is preferred by the Kathodi males. Before that only 35 per cent male prefer synthetic and 65 per cent prefer cotton fabrics.

(ii) Colours Preferred in the Upper Garment

No change is reported by the people. During the field visit it is observed that from 6 decade till today no change in the colour preference occurred.

(iii) Fabric print of Upper garment

This aspect is also same given last 6 decade. No change is observed and regarding the fabric print.

II. LOWER GARMENT

The lower garment of Kathodi male tribe is similar to that of Bhil male tribe, i.e. *dhoti* and pant (trouser). The old age male prefer only *dhoti* while, middle and young people go for both the types of lower garment.

The design, length, fabric, print all are similar to that of Bhil tribe. Two decade before only *Dhoti* is worn as a lower garment and that is plain white cotton in nature.

III. COIFFURE

1. Headdress

Pagdi or turban is the Kathodi headdress. Many times they put '*Phata*' on their head instead of *Pagdi* while, is generally at the time of their fanning work.

Table-7.20: Distribution of Male Respondents for Preference of Headdress at Present

Age group	Young N=20		Middle N=20		Old N=20		Total N=60	
	No.	%	No.	%	No.	%	No.	%
Preferred	–	–	7	35	15	75	22	36.66
Not preferred	20	100	13	65	5	25	38	63.33

Table-7.20 gives a clear picture that mainly old age people prefer headdress i.e. 75 per cent, while, young ones does not prefer any phata or turban. Nearly 63 per cent Kathodi does not prefer headdress only 36 per cent go for it.

The *Pagdi* is worn by every male before 2 decade. It is considered compulsory for every married male to wear *Pagdi*. This rejection is started only from last one & half decade before.

Kathodi's *Pagdi* is of red colour and its length is 3.5 m and width is 16" only. It is smaller in length than the *Pagdi* length of Bhil tribe. Some people also wear white or other light colours also.

ORNAMENTS

Jewellery

Kathodi males does not show much interest in the jewellery. They feel that jewellery is generally women attire only few males wear some of the basic jewellery. The second reason observed behind their less interest towards jewellery is the poor economic status.

They wear only chain in the neck and long in the ear sometimes during marriage they wear *Kada* in their hands. All the jewellery is of silver metal. Few Kathodi wear white metal because of its cheapness.

No change is observed regarding the males in the jewellery since independence. The minor change is in the weight of jewellery. Previously it is of heavy weight now people prefer light weight jewellery.

Tattooing

Every Kathodi male and female member is fond of tattooing. They generally prefer because it improves their looks and is also a symbol of social status.

Tattooing is generally done on the hands, legs, palm, forehead, chin. In general it is done at the age of 4-5 years though it vary according to individual preference. It is generally done in the fairs. First of all the name is written on the hands and then different motifs such as flower, sun, dots, snake, Scorpio local *devi-devta,* etc. are made at different body parts. The colour of tattooing is green. It is painful though people love to have it as they feel that it improves their personality.

No change is reported by the Kathodis regarding the tattooing technique of body decoration since independence.

Materials used for Improving Appearance

Similar to the Bhil tribe these people also use the cosmetic material available in the local market i.e. nail polish, lipstick, ribbon, Buckol, fancy rubber bands, Powder, cream *Kajal,* etc. These people are fond of make-up. Their use is increasing day-by-day because of their increased exposure towards mass- media, cinema, etc.

In earlier times it is not so popular, simple living is preferred or in other words people are ignorant about various cosmetic items as they are not readily available but to poor connectivity with the urban areas.

Footwear

During the field visit it was observed that *chappal* and shoes are the most popular footwear among the Kathodi tribe.

Table 7.21: Distribution of Kathodi male Respondents wore different Footwears at Present

Particulars	Young N=20		Middle N=20		Old N=20		Total N=60	
	No.	%	No.	%	No.	%	No.	%
Chappal	8	40	13	65	20	100	41	68.33
Shoes	12	60	7	35	–	–	19	31.66

The Table 7.21 highlights the fact that around 68 per cent males wear *chappal* and remaining 31 per cent go for shoes. The old age people wear only *chappal* as their footwear.

Changing Trend in Footwear

In the earlier time the people generally remain bore foot during 4 decade prior some people started wearing *chappal* and later they shifted towards the shoes. The shoes are generally of plastic and rubber ones. They does not prefer the leather shoes mainly because they are costly and thus unaffordable.

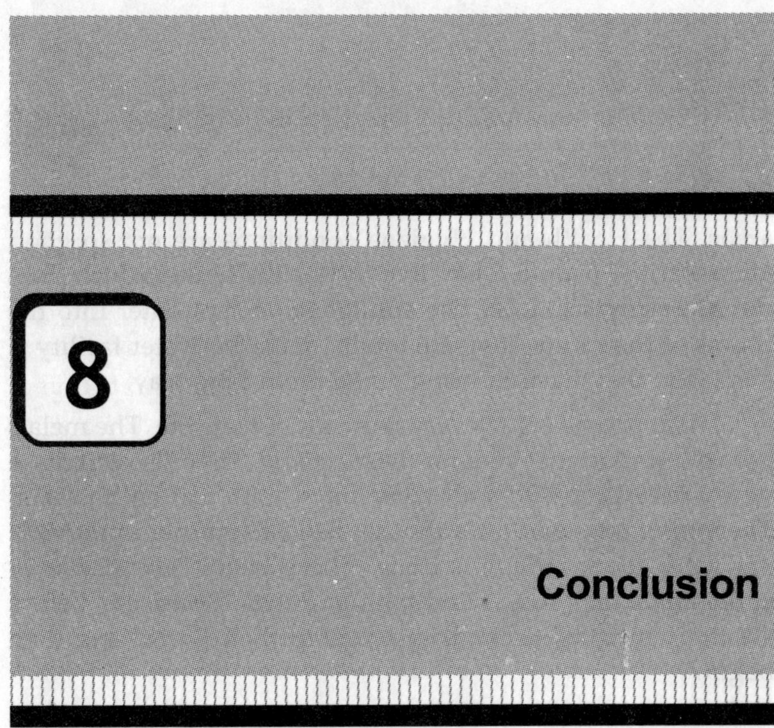

8 Conclusion

Costume is the language which tells about nature, culture, status, personality, creativity, interest and values of any individual. It provides visible index of the homogeneity and the unity of oeople. Costume includes coiffure and ornaments. Consciously unconsciously, people are at first interested in clothes and ornaments as devices for enhancing the attractiveness of the body, but gradually they develop an interest in clothes for their own sake.

Costume has been functioning as a fashioner of personality and has tended to be cultivated as an art in today's unique way to dressing which at a glance distinguish it from the other committee.

The research is done on four tribal groups of tribal sub plan area of Udaipur district i.e. Bhil, Garasia, Damor & Kathodi. Every tribe has its unique style of living. The common feature among these tribes are that they live separately on hill and do farming around their hut. These people are very rigid in following their costumes.

They prefer to live isolate i.e. away from rural, urban areas, The Health and Hygiene conditions are not so good among tribal people. They live in Kachha house which does not have any window. The sunlight does not enter into the rooms of their huts, they are totally dark. No water facility is available, they have to bring water from long way.

Tribal people enjoy every moment of their life. The mela's are very important event for these people. They also purchase new dresses for *mela* and wear them with full enthusiasm. The young boys and girls choose their life partner in the *mela* and later the marriage is done. These people are also very superstious they have blind faith in *Purvaj, Bhopa,* etc. Before starting any good work they worship their *Purvaj* and then begin.

The economic condition of tribal people is not good enough, therefore lot of services and supplies are done by government for the upliftment of these people.

Now a days the changes can be observed in the education level of these people, which bring little change in their life style and thinking tank, which reflect in their clothing also.

Major Findings

(1) The traditional costume of Bhil women is Gherdar *Ghaghra,* Kanchli and Odhi., The total fabric requirement for *Ghaghra* is 7 meter i.e. 5 m. printed & 2 m. for magji.

(2) The traditional costume of Garasia women in Gherdar_ *Ghaghra,* Jhulki and *Odhni.* For *Ghaghra* around 8-20 metre fabric is required and it is of multicolour cotton fabric. Jhulki is the upper garment which is having full sleeve and beautifully decorated with embroidery, lace and mirror work. Young girls embroider their and their friends name on the Jhulki. The *Odhni* is of bright cotton fabric, & made by 4 metre fabric. These are having floral prints.

(3) The traditional costume of Kathodi women is dhoti saree & blouse. Their Dhoti Saree is 9 m in length. This *saree* is worn in dhoti pattern therefore they does not require any other lower garment.

(4) The traditional costume of Damor women is *Ghaghra,* Blouse and *Odhni.* The *Ghaghra* is made through 3 meter fabric with knife pleats.

(5) Traditional dresses of men is *Dhoti, Kurta* and *Pheta* or *Sapha* in all the four tribes i.e. Bhil, Garasia, Damor and Kathodi. These people generally wear white colour garments.

(6) During investigation it is observed and also reported that these tribal people are very fond of jewellery. They generally wear their whole jewellery while going to the *Mela* and in marriages. The designs of each of the ornament is exclusive and they are very heavy in weight. They wear around 2-3 Kg. silver in their legs and 1 to 2 kg. in neck. Silver is used for the jewellery and gold is used only for nose pins. The two reasons are reported one is that the cost of gold is too high to purchase and secondly due to lower purchasing power gold is not available in the local market. The most common jewellery are—*Dhimna long, ogania, Hasali, Tagli, Viti, Kada, Kakona, Anwale, Pajib, Bichhudi, Horki, Chudi, Hathpal, Anurole, Murki Mangalsutra.*

(7) The tattooing is commonly preferred body decoration from last 6 decades till today in all the four tribes. They generally tattoo their name on the hand and motifs like sun, flower, moon, Scorpio, snacks, star, etc. are also made on chin, foot, forehead and chick.

(8) The tribal people are very colour loving i.e. they love bright and flourscent colours. The most colourful tribe is Garasia. These people wear colourful dresses with heavy decoration.

(9) The cotton is most preferred fabric by these tribal people. The Garasia prefer cotton fabric for *Ghaghra* and *Odhni* and *julki* is of synthetic fabric. Other tribes i.e. Bhil, Kathodi and Damor these have now shifted from cotton fabric to synthetic fabric. As synthetic is durable, the colours are fast, easy to wash. These tribal people change their clothes once or twice in a week, therefore they become very soiled and it is very difficult to clean them those dirt cotton garment. But it is quite easier to clean synthetic fabric and its colour will also remain as such therefore they had shifted to synthetic.

(10) The tribal women are very keen about their appearance and looks. They use all the cosmetic items which are available in their local market. Such as lipstick, Nailpolish, Powder, Cream, *Kajal*, etc. They also use different types of ribbons, clips, rubber, butterflies and Buckle, etc. to make different hair styles. The Bhil women use to cut their front hair which will lay on the forehead, the style is known as *Sadhna cut.*

Changing Trend in Traditional Costume

(1) In Bhil female garments it is reported that Gherdar *Ghaghra* is taken over by petticoat and pleated *Ghaghra* which require less fabric and construction is also simple. The *Kanchli* which is the traditional upper garment of Bhil female is also changed to blouse. Now a days only blouse is worn by these females. The *Odhni* has also reduced in its dimension. The shorter is preferred than the longer older one.

(2) Little change is observed in Garasia. This tribe is still following their traditional costume. Change in their lower garment is that few of them have shifted to the pleated *Ghaghra* for convenience during work. They wear this *Ghaghra* only when they do hard work at

field. Very few women started wearing blouse instead of *julki,* but they did not left their traditional *julki.* No change is reported in the *Odhni.*

(3) Some of the Damor women have shifted to saree from their traditional costume. They wear saree of right shoulder and put *palla* on their head.

(4) Kathodi women is totally shifted to the modern dress i.e. blouse & *Odhni. Very* few old women wear dhoti saree otherwise everybody has started wearing *Ghaghra. Kanchli* is not seen, ever body started wearing blouse either it is young or old.

(5) The men costume in all the four tribal group is totally changed. Only old people are wearing *dhoti, Kurta,* and *Phata* or *Sapha,* otherwise the young and middle. age people started *wearing* pant, shirt and they does not prefer any headdress.

(6) It is observed during investigation that tribal women does not know the art of stitching. Even they are unable to repair their tomed garments. Therefore they use only tailoremade garment earlier but now a days these dresses are also readily available in the local market with good designs and decoration.

(7) No change is observed in the jewellery of the tribal people. The only change observed is the weight of the jewellery i.e. weight is reduced. Now a days they prefer light weight jewellery than the earlier times. Today the artificial ornaments are also popular due to their ready availability, attractive designs, and high cost of silver. These women fulfill their erge of wearning jewellery through these artificial jewellery.

(8) Every tribal people have started wearing chappal or shoe which ever is available when they go out of their home. Traditionally they does not wear any of the footwear.

(9) Traditionally the women does not cut their hair but now they prefer hair cutting and make different hair style.

Causes of Changes in Tribal Costume

(1) Less availability of traditional costume in the local market.

(2) Cost of the traditional dress is more than the prevalent dress. It is because the fabric requirement in traditional dress is more and its construction style is dificult and time consuming which ultimately increases its cost.

(3) Tribal people have started working out of their village and came in contact with the urban people which ultimately affect their style of living and also influence their costume.

(4) In the olden time these tribal people were cut off from the rural, urban areas but now due to improved transportation facility and increased road. Connectivity bring changes in their costume and overall development.

(5) Due to education these remote areas are also developing and are also keen to adopt all those facilities which will improve their work efficiency and also their looks. Due to education these people become somewhat flexible and started adopting the changes which are fruitful and beneficial to them.

(6) The media has also bring change in life's of tribal people. In the olden times they live in remote areas where they are ignorant about the whole world. They even don't know what is happening outside from their village. But today the picture is totally changed the newspaper, radio and television are reached to their places not in individuals homes but at common or community centres. The hostels are made for the ST

students from 6th standard to 12th standard where they study, get food, clothes uniform, extra allowances and recreation facility. Generally the T.V. is provided to the hostels and the people residing near to the hostel also see the television, which will give them the various knowledge about their agriculture, animal rearing practices and health & hygiene etc.

This television bring change in the use of accessories and costume by these people. They are aware about the various brands of cosmetics available in the market. Young boys started following those dresses which are prevalent or in fashion.

(7) The various cultural exchange programmes running by the different government department such as M.L.V. Tribal Research Institute, Udaipur select the tribal groups and send these people for the cultural exchange programme at different places in India. This grand exposure to these remote people bring drastic change in their personality when they see the different tribal groups of different slates they communicate and learn a lot from each other. The group when come back and share its experience with other villagers then they are also motivated and try to do better ana also become eager to go out and see the world which ultimately bring change in their approach towards life and thus the process of change started in every area of their life. The costume comes first because whenever a person have money the wants to look good and for that he purchase new and fashionable garments which bring change in the costume.

Bibliography

Agarwal, V.S. : References to Textiles in Banana's Harshacharita, *Journal of Indian Textile History,* 1959.

Alkargi, Roshan : Ancient Indian Costumes, 1983 An Heritage Books Publication. Baden-Powell, *Handbook of the manufacturers and Arts of the Punjab,* Lahore, 1872.

B.J. Dave : Tribe Wartia, 1964.

Bairathi, Shashi : "Tribal culture, Economy and Health", *A study of Bhils of Rajasthan* (An unpublished study by Department of History and Indian culture, University of Rajasthan, Jaipur) 1993.

Bakrabarti, M. and Mukharji, D.: Indian Tribes, Saraswati Library Pub. Bidhan Sarani, Calcutta, 1971.

Bardhan, A.B. : The tribal Problem in India, Communist Party of India Publication, New Delhi, 1973.

Basu, A.R. : The Tribal Development Programme and Administration in India, National Book Organisation, New Delhi, 1985.

Bernard Roshco : The Bag Race (New York: Fank and Wagnalls, Inc. 1963).

Bhatnagar Parul : Traditional Indian Costumes and Textiles, Chandigarh, Abishekh Publication, 2003.

Bhavani Enakshi: "Folk and Tribal Designs of India", Taraparewala, Mumbai, 1974.

C. Willett Cunnington : why women wear cloth, London: Faber & Faber Ltd, 1941.

Carstairs, Morris: "The Bhils of Kotra Bhomat" *An article in Eastern Anthropologist,* Vol. VIII, 1954.

Catopadhaya, Kamaladevi: *Tribalism in India,* 1978.

Chandra, Moti : "Prachin Bhartiya Vesha Bhusha", Mumbai, 1950.

Chandra, Moti : Costumes, Textiles, Cosmetics & Coiffure in Ancient & Medival India, Delhi, 1973.

Chaudhary, Buddhadeb : Tribal Development in India Problems and Prospects, Inter-India Publication, Delhi, 1982.

Chaudhary, N.D.; Vyas, N.N.; Mann, R.S. (Ed.) : Movements of Tribals in India, Publication Scheme, Jaipur, 2000.

Col. James Tod : Annals and Antiquities of Rajasthan, Vol. I.

Das, S.T. : "Lifestyle of Indian tribal", Grain Publishing house, New Delhi, Vol. III, 1989.

Debarat, Mandal : "Life and Culture of the Bhils of Mewar". Changing face of Bhils, Shiva publishing distributors, 1998.

E. Adamson Hobel: Man in the Primitive World: An introduction to Anthropology 2nd ed.: New York: McGraw-Hill Book Co. 1958.

Edmund Bergler: Fashion and the inconcious, New York: Robert Burnner, 1953.

Elwin, Vermier : The Nagas in the Nineteenth Century, Oxford University Press, Bombay, 1969.

Elwin, Verrier : A new Deal for tribal India, 1963.

Gejur, Agnes : A History of Textile Art, 1979, p. 104.

Ghurye, G.S. : The scheduled Tribes, Popular Prakashan, Bombay, 1969.

Gupta, Shalini : Cultural Tourism and Heritage Management, Jaipur, 1994.

Havelock Ellis : Studies in the Psychology of sex IV: The Evolution of Modesty, Vol. I. (New York: Random House, Inc. 1942).

Hendl, R.S. : An account of Mewar Bhils, an article on the Journal of Asiatic, Society Bengal, 1875.

J. Marshall: Monhenjo-daro and the Indus civilisation, London, Vol. III, 1931.

Jain, Nami Chand : Bhil Bhasha, Sathiya Aur Sanskrit, Hira Bhaya Prakash Indore (M.P.) 1964.

James Laver : "Laver's Law" interview, Women's wear Daily, July 13, 1964.

James Tod : Travels in Western India, V. FLALLEN & Company, London, 1839.

Janet Harry : Traditional Textiles of Central Asia, 1978.

John, Carl Flugel : The Psychology of clothes, Hogarth Press & the Institute of Psychoanalysis, 1930.

Kamla S. Dongerkery : "The Romance of Indian Embroidery" 1951.

Karen, Baclawshi: "Agude to historic Costume, 1948.

Kay, Talwar and Kalyan Krishna : Indian Pigement Painting on Cloth, Ahmedabad, 1979.

Kramresicha, Stella : 'Kantha', Journal of Indian Society of Oriental Art, VII, 1993.

Kumar, Pramod : "Folkicons and Rituals in tribal life", Abhinav Publications, 1984.

Mahendra, B.I.: 'History and Culture of Girasia', Adi Prakashan, 1985.

Majumdar, D.N. : The Affairs of a Tribe—A Study in Tribal Dynamics, Universal Publishers Ltd., Lucknow, 1950.

Mathur, J.S.: Tribal Development Administration, Perspective on Tribal Development and Administration Hyderabad, 1975.

Mathur, L.P.: The Bhils of Western India, National Publishing House, New Delhi, 1985.

Mathur, V.B.: "Folkways in Rajasthan", Himalaya an Publication, 1986.

Meharda, B.I.: History and Culture of Girasias, Adi Prakashan, Jaipur, 1985.

Mehta Prakash Chandra, Mehta, Sonu : Cultural Heritage of Indian Tribes, Discovery Publishing House, New Delhi, 2007.

Mehta, P.C.: "Tribal Development", Shiva Publishers, 1999.

Mehta, Prakash Candra: Development of Indian Tribes, Discovery Publishing House, New Delhi, 2006.

Mehta, Prakash Chandra: Bhart-Ke-Advisai, Shiva Publishers Distributors, Udaipur, 1993.

Mehta, Prakash Chandra : Changing face of Bhils, Shiva Publishers & Distributors, 1998.

Mishra, S.N.; Singh, Bhupinder : Tribal Area Development, Aruna Printing Press, New Delhi, 1983.

Naht, Y.V.S. : Bhils of Ratanmal M.S. University Journal, Baroda, 1960.

Northrop. F.S.C. : "Cultural Values". In Anthropology Today (Ed.), A.L. Kroeber, Chicago, 1953.

Rajasthan State Archives, Bikaner, Sirohi, record, Basta No. 3, file No. 160 of 1931.

Rajora, Suresh Chandra : Social Structure and Tribal Elites, Himanshu Publications, 1987.

Ray, Niharranjan : "Introductory Address" in S.C. Dube (Ed.) Tribal Situation in India, 1972.

Rigvi, S.H.M. : Mina—The Ruling Tribe of Rajasthan. D.K. Publishers, New Delhi, 1987.

Robert, Deliege : The Bhil of western India, National, Delhi 1985.

Roy, S.C. : Bhils of Mewar, Calcutta, 1924.

Roy, Shibani; Rigvi, S.H.M. : Tribal Customary laws of North-East India, B.R. Publishing Corporation, Delhi, 1990.

Sahay, Sachidanand : "Indian Costume, Coiffure and Ornaments", Munshiram Manohar Lal Publishers Pvt. Ltd., New Delhi, 1975.

Sane, K.J. : "The Wartis", Delhi, 1979.

Sharma, B.D. : Growth Centres in Tribal Areas, Ministry of Home Affairs, Government of India, New Delhi, 1975.

Sharma, G.N. : Mewar and the Mughal Emperors, Shiv Lal Agrawal and Company (Private) Ltd, Agra, 1962.

Singh Hoshiar : Tribal Development Administration, Printwell, Jaipur, 1994.

Singh, K.S. (Ed.) : Tribal Situation in India, Indian Institute of advance studies, Simla, Vedic Index, Vol. II, 1972.

Singh, K.S.: Tribal Society in India, Manohar, New Delhi, 1985.

Sir Read, H : Art in an aboriginal society-A comment, A artist in Tribal Society, 1983.

Sirsikar, V.M. : The Rural Elite in a Developing Society, Kennikat, Washington, 1970.

Symcox, A.H.: The History of Khandeshli Bhil, 1960.

Tod, James : Annals and Antiquities of Rajasthan Vol. I-II Reprint, 1960.

Verma, S.C. : The Bhil Kills, King Publishing Home, Delhi, 1978.

Vidyarthi, L.P. and Rai, Binay Kumar : The tribal culture of India, Concept Publishing Company, 1977.

Journal

Chaturvedi, D.N. : *"Role of Bhils in the freedom struggle"*, Tribe, Vol. X, No. 1 & 2, 1986.

Chaudhari, Sankho : *"Fold and Tribal Images of India"*, (Catalogue & Bulletin), Lalitkala Academy, New Delhi, 1970.

Chauhan, B.R. : *"Tribalism"* in Tribe (especial issue on Rajasthan Bhils), Vol. X, 1975.

Chauhan, B.R. and Chelawat, D.S. : "Bhil Gavri", Tribe, Vol. VIII-No. 1, 1966.

Choudhary, N.D. Vyas, N.N. : *"Barmer : The Border district"*, Tribe, Vol. VII, No.2. 1970.

Col. Tod, James : *"Annals and Antiquities of Rajasthan"*, Vol. I-II. I960.

Das, S.T. : *"Lifestyle of Indian tribal"*, Vol. Ill Gain Publishing House, New Delhi, 1989.

Das, Shyamal : *"Veer-Vinod"*, Vol. I, Udaipur, The royal palace.

Gujati, R.K. : *"A profile of social change among the Bhils of west Khandesh"*, Tribe, June 1970, Vol. VII No. 1.

Lokhit Vikas Sansthan : *"Tribes of Rajasthan"*, (An unpublished Research Report, Sponsored by M.L.V. Tribal Research Institute).

Mahendra, B.L. : *"History and culture of the Garasia"*, Adhiprakashtan, Jaipur, 1985.

Mann, R.S. : *"Bhil economy and its problems"*, Tribe, Vol. X. 1978.

Mann, R.S. : *"Some aspects of cultural life of Damors"*, Vanyajati 1966, Vol. XIV (2), April,

Mehla, Prakash Chandra: *"Demographic Profile of Tribal"*, Tribe Vol. XXI-XXIII, January 1989 to Dec, 1991, Tribal Research Institute, Rajasthan, Udaipur, Udaipur, 1991.

National Archieves of Indian: *"Study on Bhils"*, Government of India, 1984.

National Institute of Design: *"Traditional Garments of Udaipur, Banswara and Dungarpur"*, Paldi Ahmedabad, 1992.

Shah, Dilip : *"Tribal Development: Planning and Performance"*, Kurukshetra, June, 2003.

Shah, V.M. : *"Cooperative and Tribals"*, Tribe, No. 34, M.L.V., Tribal Research, Institute, Udaipur, Sept-Dec. 1984, pp. 11-12.

Sharma, Sheela; *"Aadivasi Kala Parivartit Swarololp"* Tribe, 1988, Vol. XX, No. 1-4.

Sharma, Sheela : *"Aadivasi Kala Parivartit Swaroop"*, Tribe, Vol. XX, No. 1-4, 1988.

Sing, K.S. : *"People of India, Rajasthan"*, 1984, Vol. XXXVIII.

Singh, J.P. and Vyas, N.N. (Ed) : *"Tribal Development : Past Efforts and New Challenges"*, Tribal Research Institute, TRIBE Vol. XVIII No. 1-4 January 1986 to Dec. 1986.

Vijayanand, B. : *"Modified Fibers"*, Indian Textile Journal, Vol. 110, No. 7, 2000.

Vyas N.N. : *"A Border Tribe of Rajasthan"*, Tribe Ed. Vol. IV (1), 1967.

Vyas, Narendra : *"Bhil Nari"*, Tribe, Vol. XI, No. 2-4, 1979.

Index

L